Arthur Plantagenet

Arthur Plantagenet

Henry VIII's Illegitimate Uncle

Sarah-Beth Watkins

PEN & SWORD
HISTORY

First published in Great Britain in 2022 by
Pen & Sword History
An imprint of
Pen & Sword Books Ltd
Yorkshire – Philadelphia

ISBN 978 1 39900 061 1

A CIP catalogue record for this book is
available from the British Library.

Typeset by Mac Style
Printed and bound in the UK by CPI Group (UK) Ltd,
Croydon, CR0 4YY.

MIX
Paper from
responsible sources
FSC
www.fsc.org   FSC® C013604

Pen & Sword Books Limited incorporates the imprints of Atlas,
Archaeology, Aviation, Discovery, Family History, Fiction, History,
Maritime, Military, Military Classics, Politics, Select, Transport,
True Crime, Air World, Frontline Publishing, Leo Cooper, Remember
When, Seaforth Publishing, The Praetorian Press, Wharncliffe
Local History, Wharncliffe Transport, Wharncliffe True Crime
and White Owl.

For a complete list of Pen & Sword titles please contact

PEN & SWORD BOOKS LIMITED
47 Church Street, Barnsley, South Yorkshire, S70 2AS, England
E-mail: enquiries@pen-and-sword.co.uk
Website: www.pen-and-sword.co.uk

Or

PEN AND SWORD BOOKS
1950 Lawrence Rd, Havertown, PA 19083, USA
E-mail: Uspen-and-sword@casematepublishers.com
Website: www.penandswordbooks.com

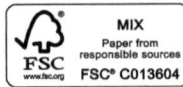

Dedication

To Jake and Shay

Contents

Dramatis Personae

The life story of Arthur Plantagenet, later known as Lord Lisle, is peppered with characters from the Tudor court to the garrison town of Calais. Listed here are some of the most referred to.

Bryan, Francis (c.1490–1550)
Lisle's lifelong friend and supporter at court. Bryan was a diplomat and one of Henry VIII's Gentleman of the Privy Chamber, later becoming Lord Justice of Ireland. He was a jouster, poet, soldier, sailor, ambassador and one of Henry's closest companions with a reputation for being a hell-raiser and a womaniser.

Botolf, Gregory
A priest and Lisle's chaplain from 1538. Responsible for the failed plot to take Calais in the name of Rome.

Cheriton, John
An unlucky mariner and merchant. Builder of Lisle's ship the *Mary Plantagenet*.

Cranmer, Thomas (1489–1556)
Supporter of the English Reformation and the first Protestant Archbishop of Canterbury during the reigns of Henry VIII, Edward VI and Mary I. He was instrumental in building the case for Henry VIII's divorce from Katherine of Aragon. Burnt at the stake by Mary I.

Cromwell, Thomas (1485–1540)
Henry VIII's chief minister, principal secretary and Lord Privy Seal. A staunch proponent of the English Reformation and in charge of the dissolution of the monasteries. Executed in 1540.

Edward IV (1442–1483)

The first Yorkist king of England from 1461–1483 and Lisle's father. Married to Elizabeth Woodville and father of ten legitimate children.

Fitzwilliam, William (c.1490–1542)

Served Cardinal Wolsey as treasurer, conducted diplomatic duties and was made vice-admiral. He was also comptroller of the royal household and keeper of the privy seal. He rose to become lord high admiral and in 1537 was made Earl of Southampton.

Henry VII (1457–1509)

The first Tudor king of England. Henry spent the early part of his life in exile until his defeat of Richard III at the Battle of Bosworth in 1485. He married Elizabeth of York, daughter of Edward IV and reigned for twenty-four years.

Henry VIII (1491–1547)

Henry VII's second son who came to the throne after his father's death in 1509. The most famous Tudor monarch and notorious for the treatment of his six wives.

Husee, John (c.1500–1548)

Husee was Lord Lisle's agent and right-hand man. He apprenticed under his father as a vintner in 1520 and joined the company in 1527. He joined the retinue of Sir Robert Wingfield the same year but transferred to Lisle's service in 1533 and is the main correspondent in the *Lisle Letters*.

Kingston, William (c. 1476–1540)

Kingston was another close friend of Lisle's and had a varied career at the Tudor court rising from sewer (server) to knight of the king's body and captain of the guard. He was the Constable of the Tower of London during the reign of Henry VIII and while Queen Anne was incarcerated.

Lisle, Honor (c. 1493–1566)

Honor married Lisle as her second husband in 1529. The daughter of Sir Thomas Grenville of Stowe in the parish of Kilkhampton, Cornwall, and Bideford in North Devon, she first married Sir John Basset in 1515.

Norris, Henry (c. 1482–1536)

Henry VIII's Groom of the Stool and influential courtier. A supporter of Queen Anne Boleyn. Executed for adultery and his supposed involvement with the queen.

Pole, Geoffrey (c. 1501–1558)

The son of Margaret Pole and Reginald's brother, he was responsible for allegations against his older brother and the Marquess of Exeter in what became known as the Exeter conspiracy.

Pole, Henry (c. 1492–1539)

Henry Pole, 1st Baron Montagu, was the eldest Pole son. He was a justice of the peace for Somerset, Dorset, Hampshire and Sussex and was present at Queen Anne Boleyn's trial. After his brother implicated him in the Exeter plot, he was executed in 1538.

Pole, Reginald (1500–1558)

Once supported by Henry VIII, he angered the king by his response to Henry VIII's divorce. Made Cardinal, he lived in Rome until Mary I's accession when she overruled his attainder. He was made Archbishop of Canterbury in 1556. He died just hours after Mary I's death.

Pole, Margaret (1473–1541)

The daughter of Edward IV's brother, George Duke of Clarence, and wife of Sir Richard Pole. As Countess of Salisbury, she was a wealthy landowner but devoted much of her life to raising Mary I. She was confined in the Tower for over two years after the Exeter conspiracy although there was little evidence against her. She was executed in 1542.

Richard III (1452–1485)

King of England from 1483 after the death of his brother Edward IV. Deposed Edward V (one of the Princes in the Tower) to take the throne. Killed by Henry VII's army at the Battle of Bosworth in 1485.

Tuke, Brian (?–1545)

Sir Brian Tuke was Cardinal Wolsey's secretary. He went on to serve Henry VIII and became treasurer of the household and Master of the King's Posts.

Whethill, Richard (c. 1465–1536)
Lord Mayor of Calais and father of Robert Whethill. The Whethills were an old Calais family and disputed Lisle's authority.

Wingfield, Robert (c. 1464–1539)
An English nobleman and diplomat originally employed by Cardinal Wolsey. He was Lord Deputy of Calais from 1526–1531 and later became mayor. A vast landowner around Calais, he fell out with Lisle over the issue of draining Wingfield's Marsh.

Introduction

The life of Arthur Plantagenet has always fascinated me. He is yet another oft mentioned but little known character in Tudor history; famously known as Edward IV's illegitimate son and for his time in Calais, but not much else. Denigrators have described him as incompetent, weak and incapable but his story is so much more complicated. Here is a man who witnessed four kings on the throne of England; one of whom was his father, another his nephew.

He was never far from court and saw the rise and fall and the comings and goings of the royal family and the nobles that surrounded them. And like them he rose from a humble position. He became vice-admiral and then Lord Deputy of Calais, a trusted and respected servant of King Henry VIII, his nephew.

The facts about Arthur's early life are scant. We owe much of what we know about Henry VIII's uncle to the seizure and preservation of the *Lisle Letters* in 1540 but they only catalogue the last phase of Arthur's life and his time in Calais. This book will rely heavily on them for that period. Muriel St Clare Byrne spent years compiling the *Lisle Letters* from over 3,000 documents into six volumes, which not only give details of Arthur's life but are an amazing insight into the religious, political, cultural and social background of 1533–40.

Lisle's correspondents were wide and varied from Henry VIII to Cromwell to some other prominent figures in Tudor history like Sir Francis Bryan, Sir Henry Norris, the Duke of Norfolk and Sir William Fitzwilliam. Others were family members like Margaret Pole, Countess of Salisbury and her son Lord Montagu and yet still more were ordinary people asking for favours, appointments or help.

The reason why some have judged Arthur as being incompetent lies in his management – or mismanagement – of Calais and his role as Lord Deputy. This book aims to show how difficult that role truly was. Not only did he have to manage a troubled town that suffered from in-fighting and personality clashes, it was also poorly funded and badly supplied by the English government. All of this took place against a background of great religious and political change.

A combination of all of these circumstances would result in Arthur's arrest and his subsequent stay in the Tower of London. That he was ever guilty of anything, there is no evidence. My hope is that this book will prove that Arthur was always the king's most loyal and trustworthy uncle.

Chapter One

The Early Years
1461–1509

Arthur Plantagenet was the illegitimate son of Edward IV, half-brother to his daughter Elizabeth of York who married Henry VII. In time he would become uncle to their children, including the most notorious Tudor monarch, Henry VIII. Arthur lived through the reigns of his father, Richard III, Henry VII and on into the reign of his nephew. Henry VIII would say that he had 'the gentlest heart living', but he would also be his downfall.

Edward IV reigned from 1461–1683, the son of Richard of York, Lord Protector of the mad king, Henry VI. Before his son became king, Richard struggled to take the throne for himself until it was agreed that he would become king on Henry's death. Yet just weeks later Richard was killed by Lancastrians at the Battle of Wakefield. His eldest son, Edward, took on his cause. On 29 March 1461, the Battle of Towton was fought between the Yorkists and the Lancastrians – England's bloodiest battle in the War of the Roses. With snow thick on the ground, the Lancaster and York armies took their positions with a blizzard swirling around them. Arrows tore through the air before the killing began. Men ripped into each other with swords and poleaxes. The fighting lasted for hours and as the fields ran red, it seemed like the Lancastrians would win, but fresh reinforcements swung the victory for York and for Edward IV.

Around 28,000 men died bloody and painful deaths. But this victory paved Edward's way to the throne and he rode into London in May 1461 as a handsome, strong and athletic king in strict contrast to the deposed, old, and often dishevelled, Henry VI. Edward would be known for his good looks, gentle nature and 'body mighty, strong and clean made'.[1] He was an imposing sight in his kingly regalia, standing over 6ft 3in tall – a trait his son would inherit – when he was crowned on 28 June 1461 in

Westminster, but his hold on the throne was a tenuous one and his private life was a matter of controversy.

Gregory's *Chronicle* states: 'men marvelled that our sovereign lord was so long without any wife, and were ever feared that he had not been chaste of his living'.[2] Edward IV, as king of England, should have made a diplomatic marriage if he had done as his councillors wanted, linking England to Burgundy, Scotland or Castile. Instead Edward surprised everyone by secretly marrying Elizabeth Woodville in 1464. The Burgundian chronicler, Lean de Waurin wrote of the king's councillor's reaction:

> they answered that she was not his match, however good and however fair she might be, and he must know well that she was no wife for a prince such as himself; for she was not the daughter of a duke or earl, but her mother, the Duchess of Bedford, had married a simple knight, so that though she was the child of a duchess and the niece of the count of St Pol, still she was no wife for him'.[3]

So Edward went against their advice and married for love. Elizabeth was born about 1437, the daughter of Sir Richard Woodville and Jacquetta of Luxembourg, at Grafton Regis, Northamptonshire, making her five years older than the king. She was a widow and had two sons, Thomas and Richard, by her first husband Sir John Grey, a Lancastrian who had fought against the Yorkists. Some said she was a witch and had ensnared the king. Others that she was a money-grabbing, politically motivated termagant but regardless of what others thought, she was crowned as England's queen on 26 May 1465. The royal couple would go on to have ten legitimate children over a seventeen-year span, but then there was Edward's illegitimate offspring that included Arthur.

There is some controversy over Edward's love life before and after his marriage. Dominic Mancini, an Italian visitor to London, described him as:

> licentious in the extreme; moreover, it was said that he had been most insolent to numerous women after he had seduced them, for, as soon as he grew weary of the dalliance, he gave up the ladies much against their will to the other courtiers. He pursued with no discrimination

the married and unmarried the noble and lowly: however he took none by force.[4]

Sir Thomas More wrote that in his youth Edward was 'greatly given to fleshly wantoness',[5] but by the time he was king his:

> greedy appetite was insatiable, and everywhere all over the realm intolerable. For no woman was there anywhere, young or old, rich or poor, whom he set his eye upon ... but without any fear of God, or respect of his honour, murmur or grudge of the world, he would importunely pursue his appetite, and have her, to the great destruction of many a good woman.[6]

Polydore Vergil writing after 1505 in his *Anglica Historia* suggested that Edward had even upset the Earl of Warwick by seducing women in his household:

> and yt caryeth soome colour of truthe, which commonly is reportyd, that king Edward showld have assayed to do soome unhonest act in the earls howse; for as muche as the king was a man who wold readyly cast an eye upon yowng ladyes, and loove them inordinately.[7]

Early biographers seem to credit the handsome king as a womaniser but yet the actual proof of his taking of women, using their bodies and breaking their hearts is exceedingly slim.

At least three mistresses are mentioned in connection with the king – one of whom being Arthur's mother: Elizabeth Lucy, Eleanor Talbot and Elizabeth 'Jane' Shore. More referred to them as 'one the merriest, another the wiliest, the third the holiest harlot'.[8] Presumably he was referring to Lady Eleanor Talbot as the holiest, Elizabeth Lucy as wily and he reiterated that 'the merriest was ... Shore's wife'. Shore is the only mistress that is named.

Sir George Buck, a writer and historian, is most famous for his history of Richard III that was still in draft form at his death in 1622 and would not be published until 1979. In it Buck wrote:

I shall not need to intimate how amorous and wanton this king was, his many mistresses ... he kept in several private places; whereof the most famous was Catherine de Clarington, Elizabeth Wiatt alias Lucy, Jane Shore, the Lady Eleanor Talbot.[9]

He mentions Catherine de Clarington (Clarendon), a fourth mistress about whom nothing is known, and also Jane Shore, as More had done, who was presumed to have been Edward's mistress from around 1470 until the king's death. Although there is evidence for her existence often being cited as 'Shore's wife', there is little actual proof of her affair with Edward IV.

Jane Shore was actually Elizabeth Lambert, born around 1445, the daughter of John Lambert, a London merchant. In 1468 she married the goldsmith William Shore, who was around fifteen years older than her, but it was not a happy marriage. It appears she stayed with him for three years, though their marriage was never consummated. She appealed to the Bishop of London for an annulment, Shore being:

so frigid and impotent that she, being desirous of being a mother and having offspring, requested the official of London over and over again to cite the said William before him to answer her ... seeing that the said official refused to do so, she appealed to the apostolic see.[10]

On 1 March 1476 the Pope declared her marriage null and void. In the Patent Rolls for December 1476, Edward gave William Shore his protection and some have taken this as an indication that it must have been around this time that Jane was the king's mistress.

It was said by More that she was the mistress that Edward had loved and:

Proper she was and fair ... yet delighted not men so much in her beauty, as in her pleasant behaviour. For a proper wit had she, and could both read well and write, merry of company, ready and quick of answer, neither mute nor full of babble, sometimes taunting without displeasure and not without disport ... where the king took displeasure, she would mitigate and appease his mind; where men were out of favour, she would bring them in his grace; for many that highly offended, she obtained pardon.[11]

But what More based this on and where he got his information is anyone's guess and he only referred to her as Shore's wife, not recalling her first name.

The historian John Ashdown-Hill posited that the name Jane rather than Elizabeth came about when the playwrights Beaumont and Fletcher used her as a character in their 1609 production of *Knight of the Burning Pestle*. At the time they knew her only as Mistress Shore and so gave the character the name Jane, which has stuck forever. However the 1603 Stationer's Register has an entry for a ballad by William White 'The Lamentacon of Mistres Jane Shore', so her name and her story must have been relatively well known despite there not being any tangible records.

Another of Edward's mistresses, Eleanor Talbot, was the daughter of John Talbot, 1st Earl of Shrewsbury, and his wife, Margaret Beauchamp. She was of noble stock with both of her parents being descended from Edward I. In 1449, Eleanor married the 28-year-old Sir Thomas Butler (or Boteler), at the tender age of 13 and went to live with his parents at Sudeley Castle in Gloucestershire. She was widowed around 1460 and soon after caught the king's eye. It is believed that he promised to marry her and even went as far as arranging a secret wedding ceremony, most likely to get her into bed. Although they were distantly related, there would have been no impediment to such a marriage and Edward, of course, would later re-enact a similar scenario with Elizabeth Woodville. As we shall see, Eleanor's relationship with the king would also become politically significant after Edward's death.

History tells us enough about Eleanor Talbot and Elizabeth 'Jane' Shore to know that neither of them were Arthur's mother, although it is claimed that Lady Eleanor may have had a son, Edward de Wigmore or Giles Gurney, that grew up secretly in a convent. The woman that stands out as Arthur's mother is Elizabeth Lucy, but again there are problems of proof and evidence that such a woman – of that name – even existed.

Thomas More, in his history of Richard III written around 1513 but not published until the 1540s, makes the first mention of Arthur's mother. He recounted a conversation when Edward supposedly told his own mother, Cecily Neville, that Elizabeth 'is a widow and hath already children, by God's blessed lady, I am a bachelor and have some too; and so each of us hath a proof that neither of us are like to be barren'. He goes on to say:

Whereupon dame Elizabeth Lucy was sent for. And albeit that she was by the king's mother and many other put in good comfort, to affirm that she was ensured unto the king, yet when she was solemnly sworn to say the truth, she confessed that they were never ensured. Howbeit, she said his grace spake so loving words unto her, that she verily hoped he would have married her; and that if it had not been for such kind words, she would never have showed such kindness to him, to let him so kindly get her with child.[12]

The *Chronicle of England* states when Edward wanted to marry Elizabeth Woodville, his mother said he was already pre-contracted to an Elizabeth Lucy who had already had his child. Thomas More also echoed the name of Elizabeth Lucy, pointing out that Richard III, before he became king, told Doctor Ralph Shaa to preach a sermon where the gathered crowd heard him say: 'the children of King Edward the Fourth were never law fully begotten, forasmuch as the king (living his very wife, dame Elizabeth Lucy) was never law fully married unto the queen their mother'.[13] Shaa refuted all other claims to the throne stating 'no certain and uncorrupted lineal blood could be found of Richard, duke of York, except in the person of the said Richard, duke of Gloucester'.[14]

It seems that several chroniclers carried on with this story, and that those like Hall and Holinshed, were actually mistaken in the identity of the woman who could have had a pre-contract with Edward IV.

Buck, in his *History of the Life and Reigne of Richard III*, explains more about Elizabeth Lucy:

The truth is, he was never contracted to her, though he loved her well, being of an affable and witty temper; nor did she ever alleadge that the King was betrothed to her, but that he had entangled her by sweet and tempting language; And who knoweth not credula res amor est? But true it is, he had a childe by her, which was the Bastard Arthur, called commonly (but unduly) Arthur Plantagenet, afterward made Viscount Lisle by H.8.[15]

He states that the pre-contracted lady was in fact Lady Eleanor Talbot, widow of Sir Thomas Butler. The facts are scant for any of Edward's mistresses but more is known of Lady Eleanor. She died in 1468, four years after the king's marriage to Elizabeth Woodville. Whether she was really Edward's wife is a matter for conjecture but as we will see later, it was certainly believed enough in subsequent reigns for their relationship to become an issue.

So, returning to this illusive woman who gave birth to Arthur, most have accepted Thomas More's assertion that it was Elizabeth Lucy or Lucie. But there is no evidence for the existence of an Elizabeth Lucy at the time. Buck, who amended the pre-contract story, however, gives us more detail on a possible family and mentions that her father was Wyat of Southampton (also spelt Wiatt) in his book, and here we have a connection if he had meant Wayte. In his early years Arthur was known as Arthur Wayte, and as his later letters testify, he was kin to the Waytes of Hampshire.

However, an Elizabeth is elusive. If we take it that Elizabeth Lucy was actually of the Wayte family and that Lucy may have been a married name, we can still find no evidence of an Elizabeth within the Lucy family. Anstis would later echo this, stating Arthur was the king's son 'by Eliz. the daughter of Thomas Wayte of Hampshire, the widow of Lucy'.[16] He had based his findings on the Philipot Pedigree of the Wayte family as set down in 1629 – which is not without its inconsistencies.

But any connection to Lucy is almost impossible to find. There was a Sir William Lucy of Dallington in Northamptonshire whose second wife was Margaret (née Fitzlewis), and she is rumoured to have slept with the king after her husband's death in 1460 so perhaps these authors were confused and we are discussing different women. It is possible that she spent time too in Warwick's household and was one of the women Edward abused there – as per Vergil's suggestion. However, Margaret Lucy, even if she did sleep with the king, was not Arthur's mother.

Two women are possible within the Wayte family of Hampshire that we know of; Thomas Wayte's illegitimate daughter Alice or Elizabeth (née Skillings), his wife. Another suggestion is that Elizabeth Wayte was Thomas' daughter from a first marriage and that neither her mother nor she lived long enough to appear in family wills or other records. There was an Elizabeth Wayte, daughter of Thomas Wayte, from Manningford Bohun, Wiltshire, who married Thomas Rogers, but we are concerned with the Waytes of Lee Marks and Segenworth near Titchfield, Hampshire, who also owned property at Brighstone on the Isle of Wight.

Alice Wayte was younger than Edward, who appears to have had more of a preference for older women and those that were widows. However, we don't know her date of birth and if Arthur was born later (around 1471), as will be discussed, when the king was in his late twenties, he may have taken a younger mistress. Alice had not married by the time she was mentioned in her stepmother's will of 1487 where she was left a generous bequest of household goods: a featherbed, a bolster, sheets, pillows of down, a covering for a bed of green and red, a great pot and a little pot of brass, a great pan and a little pan of brass, pewter basins, latten candlesticks, and cushions. Nothing more is known of Alice – whether she married or not – but it is possible she was Arthur's mother.

Her stepmother Elizabeth Skillings, however, is particularly interesting. She was first married to a John Wynnard, a merchant who died in 1459. She went on to marry Thomas Wayte, the father of Alice, around 1462. In a document of around the same time she is referred to as the 'kynges wydowe' – this is an unusual turn of phrase and may show a connection (and possible pre-contract) to Edward, but can also mean that she was the widow of a tenant-in-chief and unable to marry without the king's permission. This certainly came up in 1467 when an order was made:

> to assign dower to Thomas Wayte and Elizabeth his wife, late wife of John Wynarde, as for a fine paid in the hanaper the king has pardoned the trespass of the said Thomas in taking to wife Elizabeth, and her trespass in marrying him without the king's license.[17]

So Edward had some interest and control over this lady. If she had an affair with the king while married to Thomas Wayte, that would explain why Arthur carried his surname. However, it also means that if she was his mother and Edward his father, then there is no actual blood connection to the Waytes.

Of course it could also mean that Arthur was really a Wayte and not a Plantagenet. Edward did not publicly acknowledge him – that would come much later and by another king – yet there does not seem to be any question as to who Arthur's father was and at no time was it ever in doubt.

Curiously, later letters will show a connection between the Waytes and the Lacys. Could Lucy actually have been Lacy? The Lacy or Lacie family had members in Hampshire. So we might have a Wayte lady who married a Lacy – although I can find no evidence of this either. What we can say is that Arthur's mother was a Wayte from Hampshire and that at some point she had a liaison with King Edward IV.

Arthur's birthdate has also been a matter of much conjecture with dates ranging from 1461 to 1480. Muriel St Clare Byrne, editor of the *Lisle Letters*, concluded that he was born in May 1462, as Edward would have had an opportunity to meet Arthur's mother when on progress in 1461. A young woman from the Wayte family would not have been at court and so the king must have met her while he was on his travels. St Clare Byrne believed Edward's affair with Arthur's mother must have occurred before the king's marriage, but that is not necessarily true.

Her assumption was based on Edward's progress to Hampshire at the time, but the king was also in Hampshire in 1466 and nearby Southampton in 1470. If Arthur was born before his father's marriage his birthdate would be prior to 1464 with the presumption that Edward had no illegitimate children while married, but this might not be the case and Arthur's birth date could well be later. Margaret, later Countess of Salisbury, daughter of George, Duke of Clarence, the brother of kings Edward IV and Richard III, was born in 1473 and would write to him as her cousin. If they were of a similar age then, 1471 seems a more likely birth date for Arthur.

Edward IV's reign did not go smoothly and in 1469 he was in trouble when Warwick the Kingmaker imprisoned him in a bid to make his younger brother, George, Duke of Clarence, the rightful king. The country was plunged into turmoil and Edward fled to Bruges in October 1470. If Edward's mistress and Arthur's mother had been at court and followed Edward when he fled from England (which is highly unlikely), he could have been born in Bruges. Calais is oft quoted as his place of birth but it is unsubstantiated. St Clare Byrne made no mention of his place of birth in the *Lisle Letters*. Lille has also been mentioned but I can find no source or reason why. There were no inhabitants of Calais with the name Wayte or Waite, although there was a Thwayte so it is more likely that given his family were from Hampshire, that he was born there. His mother, as we have said before, was probably not a court lady and his conception and birth would have occurred where she lived.

Edward returned to England in March 1471, still fighting for his right to the throne. At the Battle of Barnet, Lancastrians led by Warwick were defeated and the king-maker slain. The Battle of Tewkesbury saw a further Lancastrian defeat and Henry VI's son Edward, Prince of Wales, was killed and Queen Margaret of Anjou captured. Not long after, Henry VI, who had been living in the Tower of London, was found dead, likely murdered.

Given that Edward was absent from England from October 1470 – March 1471, Arthur could not have been conceived during this time; however, he could have been born while the king was away and this may be the reason why he was not acknowledged. It has been suggested that he could have been conceived while Edward was separated from his wife prior to his departure from England and we know he was near Hampshire in April and May of 1470, giving Arthur a possible birthdate of February – March 1471.

The first mention we have of a royal bastard is in a tailor's bill dated 1472 from Mr Lovekyn. Of course this may not be Arthur, but there is no evidence of any other illegitimate child at the time. The amounts spent on a coat of black velvet, a gown of black and a gown of russet for him are similar to that for the 2-year-old Prince Edward, lending support to an earlier birthdate.

The tailor's bill was paid in January 1477. Mentioned in Scofield's book on Edward IV, he suggests these were clothes for a royal wedding, the marriage of Richard Duke of York (one of the Princes in the Tower) to Anne Mowbray, although the black gown and coat could have been mourning clothes for the funeral of Princess Margaret who died at 8-months-old and was buried in Westminster Abbey in December 1472.[18]

There is much discussion around other illegitimate children of Edward IV. One commonly referred to as Elizabeth, but later established as Margaret, was born around 1462 and has been put forward as Arthur's sister. Given that Arthur was probably born in 1471 during the king's marriage and she had no known connection to the Waytes, they were not likely siblings. Margaret married Thomas Lumley, 'and that the advancement of Lumley to be Lord was by marriage of a bastard daughter of King Edward IV'.[19] In the patent roll entry of 10 March 1479, William Dudley, Bishop of Durham, granted a licence that refers to her as such. Margaret married in 1476 so she must have been born to one of Edward's early mistresses, before the king's marriage if she really was his daughter.

Her mother could be the Margaret Lucy nee Fitzlewis mentioned above, who was considering remarrying two years after her husband's death leaving a time in her life where she could have been the king's mistress. She later had a son called John Wake who died soon after his birth in 1466. Her tomb refers to her as Margaret, the late wife of Sir William Lucy, rather than Margaret Wake so it is uncertain whether she ever married the child's father.

We can't be sure who Margaret Lumley's mother was but Edward definitely took an interest in her which lends weight to her being his daughter. Unusually, the patent roll entry mentioned above enabled Margaret and her husband Thomas to inherit three manors on the death of Thomas' grandfather, rather than after the death of his father, George.

There is even more evidence for Margaret's paternity through the dispensation required for her son Richard Lumley to marry Anne Conyers. Anne was the daughter of John Conyers and Anne Neville, and more importantly they shared descent from Ralph Neville and Joan Beaufort meaning they were related in the third and fourth degree. Ralph Neville and Joan Beaufort were Anne's great-grandparents and Richard's great-great-grandparents.

Their dispensation was granted in 1489 by the Bishop of Ostia (a future Pope) but an entry made by the Archbishop of Rotherham shows that originally the dispensation only referred to consanguinity in the fourth degree and the papal authorities in Rome had to issue a second letter confirming their relationship was also in the third degree, which was ratified by the Archbishop of York on 1 September 1489 allowing the couple to marry.

Apart from Arthur, Edward appears to have no other illegitimate sons, only daughters. There was Grace – mother unknown – who was on Elizabeth Woodville's funeral barge in 1492. That's all we know of her, just one mention and nothing else. Isabel Mylbery is another daughter we know next to nothing about. Her arms 'per bend purpure (or murrey) and azure, in fess a rose between two demi lions passant guardant facing sinister, all argent'[20] are shown in an heraldic manuscript of 1510 possibly granted by Sir Thomas Wriothesley, Garter King at Arms. The rose is the white rose of York. The description says 'educata ut fert[ur] pre Regem E[dwardum] iiij' — brought up, it is said, by Edward IV. She married 'John Audley, brother of James, Lord Audley', as shown in their coat of arms in the same manuscript. Her husband's father was John Tuchet, 6th Baron Audley – a man who was close to Edward and became Richard III's Lord High Treasurer.

There is also mention of another daughter, Mary, the wife of one Henry Harman, clerk of the King's Bench. The only mention we have of her is in the 1574 Kent visitation:

> Harman Clarke of ye Crowne vnto H: 7 … This man [Henry Harman] was H: 7 man to whome he gaue the clarkeship of the Crowne and with allgaue him the Crest belowe, depick[t]ed one his armes which Crist was giuen him after hee had maried with E: 4 daughter.[21]

Although the visitation didn't mention it, his will would later give her first name.

Whether Arthur had any contact with his half siblings would be a matter of conjecture. We do know in later years there was no proof of him having any contact with them, especially any one that may have been rumoured to be his sister so it is likely that his mother – the illusive Elizabeth Lucy – only ever had one child by the king.

If Arthur spent any time as a child at court, he may well have had an education like the Prince of Wales, Edward's eldest son. The day started with prayer followed by breakfast and then a morning of 'virtuous learning as his age shall now suffice to receive'.[22] After a midday meal there was more learning, such as Latin and French, and only after an evening meal and more prayer would he be allowed 'honest disports'. There were places at court for the young 'henchmen' – sons of nobles – who also gained an education as well as learning to joust, wear armour and fight. These are skills that Arthur definitely learnt, but his childhood years are shrouded in mystery and we can't say for certain where he was at this time.

Edward IV died suddenly in April 1483. He had gained weight and given up the sports of his youth, but he was still a healthy, middle-aged man and no one expected his sudden death, nor the tumult of political upheaval that occurred after his demise. His eldest son, Edward, succeeded him with his brother Richard, Duke of Gloucester, as Protector. But as we know, Richard was not content with just being his nephew's protector and the boy who should have been crowned as Edward V, and his younger brother Richard, were imprisoned in the Tower of London.

The Duke of Gloucester became Richard III, England's new monarch and he would do anything to legitimise his claim to the throne. In order to take the crown it is thought that he claimed that his brother Edward IV was illegitimate, but did not pursue this line of reasoning in deference to his mother, whom he was effectively branding an adulteress. Cecily Neville must have been hurt by this accusation and in her will she mentioned twice that Richard of York was the father of Edward IV, so there would be no question around his parentage.

Instead, Richard claimed that Edward's marriage to Elizabeth Woodville had been invalid due to the king's previous commitment to Eleanor Talbot. Philippé de Commynes, a diplomat who served at both the French and Burgundian courts and who had met Edward IV in exile, wrote:

> The Bishop of Bath and Wells (Robert Stillington) revealed to the duke of Gloucester that King Edward, being enamoured of a certain English lady promised to marry her provided he could sleep with her first and she consented. The bishop said that he had married them and only he and they were present. He was a courtier so did not disclose this fact and helped to keep the lady quiet, and things remained like this for a while. Later King Edward fell in love again and married the daughter of an English knight, Lord Rivers.[23]

Richard III was informed of the pre-contract by the bishop in 1483. He would go on to assert that Lady Eleanor Talbot had married Edward in 1461 – John Ashdown-Hill believed the date to be 8 June – and she is mentioned in the 1484 *Titulus Regius* (the Royal Title), that set forth Richard III's claim to the throne:

> the said King Edward was and stoode marryed and trouth plyght to oone Dame Elianor Butteler, doughter of the old Earl of Shrewesbury, with whom the saide King Edward had made a precontracte of matrimonie, longe tyme bifore he made the said pretensed mariage with the said Elizabeth Grey.[24]

Since both Edward and Eleanor were dead, there was no one to refute the claim.

The only other mistress we hear of after Richard seized the throne is Elizabeth 'Jane' Shore. Her annulment is documented as is reference to her time in Ludgate prison in 1483 after Edward's death, plus a later marriage. She was imprisoned for immorality by the Lord Mayor of London. Many have taken this to refer to her time with the king but it was actually for her clandestine relationship with Lord Hastings.

More wrote she took her penance well. Richard III:

caused the Bishop of London to put her to open penance, going before the cross in procession upon a Sunday with a taper in her hand. In which she went in countenance and pace demure, so womanly, and albeit she were out of all array save her kirtle only, yet went she so fair and lovely, namely while the wondering of the people cast a comely rud in her cheeks (of which she before had most miss) that her great shame won her much praise among those that were more amorous of her body than curious of her soul.[25]

Hastings was a loyal supporter of Richard III, but on 13 June 1483 the new king accused Hastings and two other council members of having committed treason by conspiring against his life with the Woodvilles and Jane Shore, who was accused of acting as a go-between. Hastings was executed. After her spell in Ludgate Prison, Elizabeth/Jane went on to marry Richard III's solicitor, Thomas Lynom, although the king tried to dissuade him. In a letter to John Russell, the king asked the chancellor to try to prevent the marriage but if that didn't work, to release her from prison into her father's care. They were duly married and she eventually had the child she so longed for, the child she had not been able to have during her first marriage.

But where was Arthur while history unfolded? He was most likely with his mother's family, as being at court as the son of the last king could have been a dangerous place to be. Elizabeth Woodville's legitimate sons, Edward and Richard, were last seen playing at the Tower in the summer of 1483. What happened to them after that will always remain a mystery and be heavily debated.

Technically an illegitimate son could not inherit the crown as it was decreed that an English king 'must not be begotten in adultery or incest', and that 'he who was not born of a legitimate marriage'[26] could not succeed to the crown. William the Conqueror, however, had done so by using force to assert his claim. But Arthur was not the head of a fighting force, he had no army to command and was not a political pawn. At this time in his life, around the age of 14, he was happy to remain in the background.

Others were not so content. Queen Elizabeth had been in sanctuary after her husband's death but she had managed to conspire with Henry Stafford, 2nd Duke of Buckingham, and Lady Margaret Beaufort to usurp Richard III and place Henry Tudor on the throne. The Duke of Buckingham was instrumental in Richard's king-making and had organised his coronation in July so his involvement in what came to be known as the Buckingham Rebellion of 1483 came as a shock to the new king.

In October, Buckingham was involved in a well-organised plan to replace Richard with Henry Tudor. Henry's father Edmund was the illegitimate son of Owen ap Tudor, husband of Catherine de Valois, the widow of Henry V. Through his mother Lady Margaret Beaufort, he was descended from John of Gaunt, the Duke of Lancaster and fourth son of Edward III and his third wife Katherine Swynford. It was through this maternal line that he claimed his right to the throne – a tenuous claim that did nothing to dissuade Lady Beaufort from raising her son in the absolute belief that he was the true king of England.

Henry Tudor was currently in exile in France but the plan was to land along the south coast of England with an army of mercenaries, meet up with Buckingham and his rebels and march for London. Eight days before the planned rebellion, some over-eager rebels stormed the city and were met by the Duke of Norfolk and his men. Buckingham was miles away in Wales and Henry, who had sailed for England, reached Poole but sailed onto Plymouth due to bad weather. A band of soldiers tried to trick him into believing Buckingham had triumphed but Henry, sensing a plot to capture him, sailed back to Brittany, his plans postponed.

Buckingham's army deserted and the duke was forced to hide in the house of one of his men, Ralph Bannister (or Banastre) of Lacon Hall, near Wem in Shropshire. Bannister betrayed him to John Mytton, the Sheriff of Shropshire, for a £1,000 reward. On 2 November, All Souls Day, he was beheaded in the marketplace at Salisbury. Afterwards, Richard III wrote of Buckingham that he was 'the most untrue creature living'.[27]

Buckingham had been the figurehead of the rebellion but behind him was Henry Tudor's mother, Lady Margaret Beaufort, and her ally Bishop Morton of Ely. The following January, Lady Beaufort was stripped of her estates and titles for her part in the conspiracy and forced to live under house arrest in the care of her husband, Lord Stanley.

At the same time Elizabeth Woodville's lands were also seized and her marriage to Edward IV declared bigamous, as we have seen above because Richard III believed that his brother had been married to Lady Eleanor Talbot. Her children were now illegitimate. Richard III swore he would not harm her daughters and they returned to court in March 1484.

Richard's reign, however, would not last long. The Battle of Bosworth on 22 August 1485 was a defining moment in history, when the Plantagenet dynasty ended and the Tudor began, ending the Wars of the Roses. Henry Tudor, returned to England, landing at Mill Bay near Milford Haven on 7 August 1485 with his small army. He moved through Wales recruiting men to his cause and continued the march through Shrewsbury towards London in his bid to seize the crown from Richard III. It would be an amazing victory for such an untested young man. Richard III had years of military experience and an army of 12,000 trained men and he held no fear he could possibly lose against this upstart. Holding the king's white boar standard high, Richard's troops engaged Henry and his men close to Market Bosworth in Leicester. The fighting was fierce and bloody.

As the battle continued the Stanleys, the family into which Lady Margaret Beaufort had married, watched on from their vantage point, taking neither side but with much needed extra troops who would shift the battle in Henry's favour. Henry moved away from the centre of the fighting with his close bodyguard – some think to reach the Stanleys to urge them to fight in his favour.

Richard III, saw a chance to take him down. Vergil wrote:

King Richard understood, first by espials [observation] where Earl Henry was far off with a small force of soldiers about him, then after drawing nearer he knew it perfectly by evident signs and tokens that it was Henry, wherefore all inflamed with ire he struck his horse with spurs and runneth out of the one side without the vanwards against him.[28]

Richard III tried to reach Henry to end the battle but the Stanleys, seeing the king separated from his troops, gave chase and he was unseated from his horse, blows reigning down upon him until the fatal strike smashed into his helmet, knocking off his gold crown. Tales tell that Lord Thomas Stanley found it under a hawthorn bush and placed it on Henry's head, crowning him in the field. Richard III's body was stripped bare, slung over a horse and taken to Leicester. Henry VII ordered that his corpse be left on display to prove his demise.

Although he is not listed in the records it is quite possible that Arthur was at the Battle of Bosworth in 1485 and recent finds have uncovered a badge thought to be of his livery. This identification is not without its problems. It is believed to be a version of Edward IV's fetterlocked falcon with its head to the rear suggesting illegitimacy, but could also be an eagle with a serpent in its beak – a symbol used by the Childe/Blount family. As far as we know Arthur used the broom plant for his seal – planta genista – when he began using Plantagenet as a surname around 1511, but St Clare Byrne mentions in the *Lisle Letters* that after he was knighted he used the falcon and an open fetterlock. However this was many years after Richard III's defeat.

Henry Tudor was crowned the rightful king of England on 30 October 1485 at Westminster, knowing he would marry Arthur's half-sister, Elizabeth. Back in December 1483, in the cathedral of Rennes, Henry Tudor had sworn an oath promising to marry Elizabeth of York and this may have been what saved Arthur if he had fought on the wrong side during the battle of Bosworth. He was family and posed no threat to the new king, but Henry VII was also eager to establish peace. His first proclamation read:

Henry, by the grace of God, king of England and of France, Prince of Wales, and Lord of Ireland, strictly chargeth and commandeth, upon pain of death, that no manner of man rob or spoil no manner of commons coming from the field; but suffer them to pass home to their countries and dwelling-places, with their horse and harness. And, moreover, that no manner of man take upon him to go to no gentleman's place, neither in the country, nor within cities nor boroughs, nor pick no quarrels for old or new matters; but keep the king's peace, upon pain of hanging.[29]

Yet Henry took the possibility of Edward IV having married Lady Eleanor Talbot seriously. Richard III's *Titulus Regius* was repealed by the king in November 1485 and all mention of Lady Eleanor's name erased from history. Copies of the act were ordered to be destroyed:

> that the said act, record and enrolment be taken and removed from the roll and records of the said parliament of the said late king, and burnt and entirely destroyed.[30]

Of course a copy did survive which we can read today, but Henry VII did his utmost to destroy any evidence that Edward had been married prior to his marriage to Elizabeth Woodville. If Edward had married Lady Eleanor then his marriage to his queen was bigamous and would illegitimise their children. When Henry married Elizabeth of York at Westminster Abbey in 1486, as he had sworn to do; the Houses of Lancaster and York were finally united but any whiff of his wife's illegitimacy had to be eradicated.

Now it was safer for Arthur to be at court. He held a position in his half-sister's household from at least October 1501. In Elizabeth's Privy Purse expenses, from 1502 to 1503, he heads the household list above William Denton, carver, with two entries:

> Item to Master Arthur for a year ended by Michaelmas last past £26. 13s. 4d.

> Item to the same Mr. Arthur for a quarter ended at Christmas last past £6. 13s. 4d.[31]

To have such a high position in her household, it is likely that he rose from the position of a page or groom. It is possible he was previously in Lady Margaret Beaufort's household while she was in Calais prior to his appointment as she wrote to her son Henry VII on 26 July 1501:

> And where your Grace shewed your pleasure for … the Bastard of King Edward's, sir, there is neither that nor any other thing I may do by your commandment, but I shall be glad to fulfil to my little power, with God's grace.[32]

Lady Beaufort mentions in the same letter that she has 'business within these parts', but it is not known what she was doing in Calais. It may be that she was purchasing goods for her ambitious drainage project at Boston, Lincolnshire. However, this reference may have led to the often quoted Calais as Arthur's birthplace.

Arthur was not the only one who spent time in Lady Beaufort's employ or care. His cousin, Lady Margaret, also stayed with her before her marriage to Sir Richard Pole, and her subsequent employment as governess to the Princess Mary in 1520. Margaret's brother Edward Plantagenet, 17th Earl of Warwick, is also thought to have been housed there for a time. Warwick's story is a sad one and shows just how dangerous it was to be a young claimant to the throne. He was barred from the succession due to his father, the Duke of Clarence's attainder, but young Warwick was still of royal blood and had some supporters, albeit mostly rebels.

During Richard III's reign he spent some time in Anne Neville's household. Mancini reported that he gave orders that the son of the Duke of Clarence, his other brother, then a boy of 10 years old, should come to the city and commanded that the lad should be kept in confinement in the household of his wife.

He was also at Sheriff Hutton castle but when Henry VII came to the throne, he had Warwick housed in the Tower of London. He was joined there in time by Perkin Warbeck, the infamous pretender to the crown, who claimed he was Richard of York, one of the Princes in the Tower, who had been spirited away to Europe after his brother had been murdered.

In 1499, both Warwick and Warbeck were involved in a foiled escape plot. Warbeck was executed on 23 November 1499 and Warwick was beheaded on Tower Hill on the 28th. With his death, the legitimate male line of the House of Plantagenet ended. Some believed that Warwick did not deserve his death and was led astray, even going as far to say he had a mental disability. The chronicler Edward Hall felt that Warwick's long imprisonment 'out of all company of men, and sight of beasts', had affected him 'in so much that he could not discern a goose from a capon'.[33]

So why did Arthur become closer to the royal family at this point? With Warwick and Warbeck gone, there were no more legitimate Yorkist claimants to the throne. By giving Arthur formal recognition as Edward's *illegitimate* son, he could keep him close as an ally and not an enemy.

Elizabeth of York died in 1503 and Arthur appears in her burial expenses being given five yards of cloth for his mourning livery and six yards for his two servants. His role again is not listed, but he appears after the first entry of Master Confessor and is followed by Sir Ralph Verney and William Denton, both carvers. He appears next in Henry VII's household accounts with a quarterly wage of £6. 13s. 4d, the correct wages for a Squire of the Body, although this isn't stated in the accounts. However, he is listed as such in Henry VII's funeral accounts, where he is allocated nine yards of material for his mourning attire and nine yards for his three servants.

Henry VII's act for the regulation of his household states that, the (e)squire of the body ought to array the King and unarray him', and 'no man else to set hand on the king'.[34] He was also to sleep on a pallet in the king's chamber if needed, or keep the chamber door until the king was asleep and to be ready to serve him at his 'uprising'. The position was one of close proximity to the king and only given to those found honourable and trustworthy. That Arthur had been given such a position shows he was held in high esteem.

Henry VII died on 21 April 1509. There was a delay in announcing his death but on the 24th, Prince Henry rode from Richmond to the Tower of London and was proclaimed king. It was a role that should have fallen to his elder brother Arthur, who had died at Ludlow Castle in April 1502. Henry instead was crowned in the morning of 24 June, along with his new bride, the Spanish princess, Katherine of Aragon, daughter of King Ferdinand II of Aragon and Queen Isabella I of Castile. The Archbishop of Canterbury conducted the service. Henry VIII was anointed and crowned closely followed by Katherine, the new queen of England.

Several days of celebration, feasting and jousting followed. As Edward Hall commented in his Chronicle:

> To further enhance the triumphal coronation, jousts and tourneys were held in the grounds of the palace of Westminster. For the comfort of the royal spectators, a pavilion was constructed, covered with tapestries and hung with arras cloth. And nearby there was a curious fountain over which was built a sort of castle with an imperial crown on top and battlements of roses and gilded pomegranates.

Its walls were painted white [with] green lozenges, each containing a rose, a pomegranate, a quiver of arrows or the letters H and K, all gilded.[35]

Sometime after the king's death Arthur transferred to Henry VIII's household, most likely in the same role, and appeared in the King's Book of Payments through June 1509–April 1515 with a wage of £6. 13s. 4d per quarter.

Soon he would also appear for the first time as Arthur Plantagenet. We know that Arthur used the surname Wayte in his early years and given that Henry VII gave him a place in his household, he may have been using the Plantagenet surname before it is first recorded.

The Plantagenet surname is originally linked with Count Geoffrey of Anjou, the father of Henry II, from whom Edward IV was descended, who used the broom plant – planta genista – as a heraldic emblem as Arthur did, although it doesn't appear that Geoffrey actually used the name. Arthur's grandfather, Richard, Duke of York, revived the surname and is mentioned as Richard Plantagenet in the Parliamentary Rolls of 1460. His son Edward IV didn't use it himself but did refer to his nephew as Edward Plantagenet. The surname has become synonymous with royal bastards, but apart from Richard III's illegitimate daughter Catherine, there is no evidence of its actual use as a surname prior to Arthur and may have been given to him by Henry VII to underline his connection to the royal family.

Because now Arthur was firmly in place at his nephew – King Henry VIII's – side.

Chapter Two

The King's Uncle
1510–1532

The early years of Henry VIII's reign were an exciting time for the young king. He had been kept cloistered by his father after the death of his older brother Arthur, and now he could finally fill his days with jousting, dancing, hunting, masques and pageants. He had a select group of friends including Charles Brandon, Thomas Knyvett, Henry Guildford and Nicholas Carew. Cardinal Wolsey found them such a bad influence that he would later have them banished from court. These men were all nearer to Henry in age, being in their late teens or early twenties. Arthur doesn't appear to have been as close to the king in his revelries. He would have been at least 40 by now and perhaps as the king's uncle too, he wasn't quite part of the 'in' crowd, but he was a valued member of the royal family and for the next few years Henry would reward him for his loyalty.

Henry loved his jousting and it was inevitable that Arthur would join him at a tournament. He appeared at the Maying festival and joust at Greenwich in 1510, when he answered Edmund Howard's challenge. Over four days, 23 and 27 May, 1 and 3 June, he only jousted once – possibly because of his age – whereas the younger men fought several times each day. Some historians have credited Arthur as being the man who taught Henry to joust, but given that this is the only occasion where he is recorded as taking part in a tournament that is unlikely.

One of the men who jousted with Arthur was William Kingston, his business partner and lifelong friend. Born in 1476, he was of a similar age to Lisle. On 25 July 1510 they were granted a licence to export 2,000 kerseys (woollen cloth) free of customs duty from London and Southampton. Kingston was at the time another esquire for the body and these grants were often perks of the job. He would go on to become Constable of the Tower of London from 1524 and gain infamy for caring for his most famous prisoner, Anne Boleyn.

Arthur married Edmund Dudley's widow, Elizabeth Grey, the daughter of Edward Grey, 1st Viscount Lisle and Elizabeth Talbot, who would later became 6th Baroness Lisle, on 12 November 1511. As a first marriage, wedded life came quite late to Arthur. If we surmise he was born in 1471 then he had left finding a bride until he was 40 and so this might have been more of an arrangement or suggested match. Dudley was Henry VII's advisor who, along with Richard Empson, was executed for constructive treason on 17 August 1510 – the first executions of Henry VIII's reign. The day after the wedding Arthur was granted some of the Dudley lands in Lancashire, Dorset and Sussex that had returned to the crown as part of Dudley's attainder. He became stepfather to Elizabeth's three children, John, Andrew and Jerome. Edward Guildford would go on to buy the wardship of Arthur's stepson, John Dudley, although this was a matter of dispute, with Arthur preferring to keep it in the family.

Arthur was admitted to Lincolns Inn in 1511 when it was noted he was a knight and 'of the King's household', although he would not take part in a knighting ceremony until two years later. After his marriage he served on the Commission of the Peace for Hampshire on several occasions from 1512 to 1532 and would also serve as a Justice for the Peace in Sussex where his Dudley holdings were. JPs were typically local landowners appointed to keep law and order, punish offenders and ensure any government legislation was enforced in their area.

By March 1513, Arthur had risen to become a Spear of Honour – one of a select group who protected the king. In October 1509, Henry VIII established the 'company of kings spears' as started by his father. A close bodyguard, the fifty men were 'trapped in Cloth of Gold, Silver and Gold Smiths worke, and their servants richly apparelled also'.[1] Henry Bourchier, Earl of Essex was made captain with Sir John Pechy as his lieutenant, at the head of this dashing and extravagant band of brothers. Yet they were not just for show, each man was selected for his fighting skills as well as his loyalty to the king.

Arthur and his fellow spears, men like Charles Brandon, Henry Guildford and Thomas Palmer had to swear an oath of absolute allegiance:

I shall be a true and faithful subject and servant to our sovereign lord King Henry the Eight and to his heirs, Kings of England, and diligently and truly give my attendance in the room of one of his Spears and I shall be retainer to no man, person or persons of what degree or condition, whosoever he be by oath, livery, badge, promise or otherwise but only to his grace without his special licence.

I shall not hereafter know or hear of anything that shall be hurtful or prejudicial to his most royal person, especially in treason, but I shall withstand it to the uttermost of my power and the same with all diligence to me possible, disclose to the King's Highness or the Captain of the Spears or his deputy, or such other of his council as I know will discover the same unto his Grace.[2]

Interestingly, the spears were meant to be young men of noble blood. Brandon was born in 1484, Henry Guildford 1489, Richard Cornwall 1480. Their captain, the Earl of Essex, appointed to be the mentor of the young bloods was born in 1468. John Blount seems to be one of the oldest born in 1471 which would also lend weight to Arthur Plantagenet being born later than St Clare Byrne's assumption of 1461 and would make 1471 more probable.

Henry VIII had started his reign determined to wage war on France – England's ancient enemy. The Venetian ambassador described the king as 'magnificent, liberal and a great enemy of the French'.[3] The young king would soon have a more pressing need for his spears when he declared war on France, ruled by Louis XII, in April 1512.

Many of them were first deployed aboard ship in 1512 but Arthur did not become a captain until April 1513 when he was given the command of the *Nicholas of Hampton*, a ship of 200 tons. The fleet sailed for Brest but Arthur's ship was wrecked upon the rocks. It appears they were rescued as the fleet returned to Bertheaume Bay and the sailors were reassigned to other vessels. Arthur was sent home bearing a letter for the king from the Lord Admiral, Edward Howard:

Sir, I have taken all Master Arthur's folks and bestowed them in the army where I lacked by reason of death, by casualty or otherwise. And Sir, I have given him licence to go home; for, Sir, when he was in the extreme danger (and hope gone) from him, he called upon Our Lady of Walsingham for help and comfort and made a vow that an' it pleased God and her to deliver him out of that peril he would never eat flesh or fish till he had seen her. Sir, I assure you he was in marvellous danger, for it was a marvel that the ship, being with all her sails, striking full but a rock with her stam that she brake not on pieces at the first stroke.[4]

While Arthur was safely back at home, the Lord Admiral continued to fight the French. Howard had sworn he would avenge the death of his brother-in-law, Sir Thomas Knyvet, who had died at the Battle of St Mathieu the previous year. Along with Sir John Carew, Knyvet commanded the royal flagship, the *Regent* that attacked the French vessel *Marie de la Cordelière*. They were about to board the enemy ship when it blew up and both vessels were engulfed in flame, killing over 1,700 men including Knyvet.

Howard had promised he would not rest until he had his revenge, and the following April he launched an assault on the French flagship. Boarding the vessel, his own galley came adrift, leaving Howard and his men to the mercy of the enemy's sailors. Howard threw his admiral's gold whistle overboard, his symbol of rank, and was either forced or jumped to his death, drowning in the salty water, weighed down by his heavy armour. These losses made Henry VIII all the more eager to retaliate and bring war to France.

On 30 June 1513 the king landed at Calais with an army of 40,000 men. After his naval disaster, Arthur joined his nephew in his land assault on France. Henry and his men marched on Therouanne for what would become known as the Battle of the Spurs. On 16 August, the French troops were defeated at Guinegate when they fled on horseback, their spurs glinting in the sunlight. They moved on for the siege of Tournai which fell to the English on 23 September. After a mass in Tournai Cathedral on 2 October, Henry knighted many of his captains including Arthur (although, as we have seen, he was probably knighted before, but still took part in this ceremony). Henry, like Arthur had done, paid a visit to Our Lady of Walsingham on his return to give thanks for the English victory.

After the French campaign we lose sight of Arthur except when the Earl of Surrey mentions him in a dispatch to the King's Council, where he recommends him for the role of Sheriff of Hampshire; 'methink Master

Arthur to be most convenient considering that the country regards him best of any man hereabouts'.[5] He also mentions that Arthur is currently living within three miles of Portsmouth, but it is uncertain where. That he took up the position is apparent by a case in the Court of Star Chamber, that sat at Westminster, where he is mentioned in the case of Thomas Hunt of Botley who believed himself to have been wrongly indicted for letting a thief escape and had had his goods seized.

In the *Letters and Papers* there is correspondence from Viscount Lisle to the king from France in May. The embassy was to take the oath of Louis XII's successor, King Francis I. Although it is credited as being in Arthur's hand, it is not thought that he travelled to France at this time. It was Charles Brandon that actually held the title of Viscount Lisle, being created on 15 May 1513, and it is believed the missive was actually penned by Thomas Boleyn.

Henry eventually made peace with France and welcomed French ambassadors to England in 1518 when Tournai was formally returned and the Treaty of London – a non-aggression pact between Europe's major powers – was signed. Arthur was with the king as one of his gentlemen of the palace along with others such as Thomas Boleyn, John Seymour and William Fitzwilliam. The king's men were paired with each one of Francis I's courtiers to attend processions and joined the French ambassadors at the joust, feasting and dancing that followed. Hall wrote in his Chronicle:

> and all that day were the straungers feasted, and at night they were brought into the hall, where was a rock ful of al maner of stones, very artificially made, and on the top stood .v. trees, the first an Olive tree, on which hanged a shild of the armes of the Church of Rome : the .ii. a Pyneaple tree, with the armes of the Emperour : the .iii. a Roysyer with the armes of England : the .iiii. a braunche of Lylies, bearing the armes of Fraunce : and the .v. a Pomegranet tree, bearing the armes of Spayn : in token that al these .v. potentates were joined together in one league against the enemies of Christes [fayth][6]

With a good command of French, Arthur could converse freely with the ambassadors. There was much celebration over their new alliance to be cemented by the betrothal of Princess Mary to the Dauphin of France.

The Venetian ambassador reported peace was proclaimed at St Paul's and afterwards:

> the Cardinal of York was followed by the entire company to his own dwelling, where we sat down to a most sumptuous supper, the like of which, I fancy, was never given either by Cleopatra or Caligula … After supper, a mummery, consisting of twelve male and twelve female maskers, made their appearance in the richest and most sumptuous array, being all dressed alike. After performing certain dances, they removed their visors. The two leaders were the King and the Queen Dowager of France, and all the others were lords and ladies, who seated themselves apart from the tables, and were served with countless dishes of confections and other delicacies. Large bowls filled with ducats and dice were then placed upon the table for such as liked to gamble. Shortly after, the supper tables being removed, dancing commenced, and lasted until after midnight.[7]

In October there was a ceremonious send-off for the French commissioners and noblemen from the court headed by Charles Somerset, the Earl of Worcester and the king's chamberlain, who made a return visit to the court of Francis I, arriving in December. It is possible that Arthur was one of the entourage that were warmly welcomed by Francis I who laid on many entertainments including a spectacle at the Bastille.

The spectacle was followed by a day of jousting but while ambassadorial duties were carried out by senior members of the party, the younger ones, including Francis Bryan who was a close friend, decided to ride through the streets of Paris 'throwing eggs, stones and other foolish trifles at the people'.[8] When they returned home there were in for a stern rebuke from Wolsey, who called them before the Privy Council and had them banished from court. Henry was lost without his minions for company but it meant that more senior men like Arthur and William Kingston once more surrounded the king.

Charles Brandon, Viscount Lisle and the king's closest companion, had been betrothed to Elizabeth Grey, 5th Baroness Lisle and his ward, when she was just eight years old, before his scandalous marriage to the king's sister, Mary Tudor. Elizabeth Grey was the only surviving child of the late John Grey, Viscount Lisle, and had also been Thomas Knyvet's stepdaughter. More importantly for Arthur, she was his wife's niece. When she died in 1519 at the tender age of 14, her title and lands reverted to her aunt. Although Brandon would not yet give up his title, the lands were granted to Arthur and his first wife. It was a massive inheritance with property across the country in Berkshire, Devon, Cornwall, Somerset, Wiltshire, Gloucestershire, Leicestershire, Northamptonshire, Staffordshire, Warwickshire and Worcestershire. He was fast becoming a major landowner and respected member of court.

It is no surprise then that Arthur was by his nephew's side for his most famous visit to France. In 1520 he was at the Field of Cloth of Gold representing Hampshire, and was allowed his own entourage of ten people and four horses – a small amount compared to the king and queen's retinue of 5,000 people and nearly 3,000 horses. The planning for this momentous occasion had taken months of preparation and would cost £63,000 in Tudor coin – roughly £32 million in today's money.

Arthur was with the king for his private meeting with Francis who:

met in a valley called the Golden Dale which lay midway between Guisnes and Arde where the French king had been staying. In this valley Henry pitched his marquee made of cloth of gold near where a banquet had been prepared. His Grace was accompanied by 500 horsemen and 3,000 foot soldiers, and the French King had a similar number of each.

When the two great princes met proclamations were made by the heralds and officers-of-arms of both parties, to the effect that everyone should stand absolutely still – the king of England and his company on one side of the valley and the king of France with his retinue on the other. They were commanded to stand thus, completely still, on pain of death whilst the two kings rode down the valley.[9]

For the two weeks of jousting, feasting, drinking, pageant displays, wrestling, archery and diplomatic discussions, Henry stayed in a temporary palace outside the walls of Guisnes while his entourage were housed within the castle walls or in smaller tents. Henry's 'palace of illusions' was a temporary building that covered an area of 328 feet square, with four wings surrounding a central courtyard. It was built on a brick base about 8ft high and above that the walls were made of canvas painted to look like brick and stone, with high quality glass windows earning it the name of 'crystal palace' from the French. In front of a gatehouse topped with symbolic lions and Cupid stood a fountain topped by the 'the olde God of wyne called Bacchus birlyng the wyne, whiche by the conduyetes in therth ranne to all people plenteously with red, white, and claret wyne'.[10] Over 40,000 gallons of wine and 48 tuns of ale were consumed with a brewhouse set up nearby to keep the supply going.

Food and livestock were shipped over and sourced locally – everything from sheep, calves and pigs to poultry, fish and wheat. With around 12,000 people attending, there were lots of mouths to feed on both sides and food was prepared throughout the day and night. The nobility of course ate particularly well. When Francis I dined with Katherine of Aragon, a huge banquet of three courses was served including heron, cygnets, venison, peacock and quail with sweet dishes of fruit, custards and creams to follow each course. And when everyone was full there were the entertainments of dancing, plays, masques and fireworks, including a flying dragon made from canvas stretched around wooden hoops. This amazing kite flew across the sky by way of a rope tethered to a carriage that trundled around the encampment. Some said it breathed fire and its eyes blazed, so it may have been filled with fireworks and a potential fire hazard!

All of this magnificent display of wealth and kingly power was undercut by a show of military might; 300 men took part in the jousts that were organised by the Duke of Suffolk and the French Admiral, Bonnivet. Although it does not appear that Arthur took part, he must have watched the displays and cheered on his friend Sir Francis Bryan, who achieved one of the highest scores. There were displays of horsemanship to watch and sword fighting contests. Each competition pitted the English against the French – friendly matches but with a serious undertone. Even Henry and Francis had a wrestling match, but the French king outmanoeuvred Henry with a 'Breton trip' and the English king was thrown to the ground. Absolutely enraged, Henry called for a rematch but Francis laughed it off and decided it was time for dinner, leaving poor Henry seething.

Somehow, Henry managed to leave King Francis on cordial terms, but war with the French would never be far from his mind. To that end he arranged to meet Charles V, Holy Roman Emperor, and his aunt, Margaret of Savoy, at Gravelines on his way home. Arthur accompanied the king along with Francis Bryan, Nicholas Carew, Henry Guildford and William Fitzwilliam. Henry may have met with Francis and showed his commitment to the Treaty of London, but he was ever wary of the French. It would be as well to have Charles V's support and offer his in return.

Arthur continued his duties for the king once he was back on English soil. He was a carver at the Christmas celebrations in 1521 and the following year escorted his king again to greet Charles V, by now at war with France and calling on Henry's promises of support. On 29 May 1522, so soon after the camaraderie of the Field of Cloth of Gold, Henry declared war on his sworn enemy. The Holy Roman Emperor landed at Dover to be greeted by Wolsey and Henry, Arthur and other nobles rode down to Canterbury to meet him and escort him back to London. Charles V had over 2,000 people in his retinue and 1,000 horses, so progress towards the city was slow. On 6 June:

> the king and the Emperour with all their companies, marched toward London, where the citie was prepared for their entrie, after the maner as is used at a coronation, so that nothing was forgotten that might set foorth the citie. For the rich citizens well apparelled stood within railes set on the left side of the streetes, and the cleargie on the right side in rich copes, which censed the princes as they passed, and all the streetes were richlie hanged with clothes of gold, – siluer, veluet, and arras, and in euerie house almost minstrelsie.[11]

At Greenwich, Charles V was greeted by his aunt Queen Katherine and the Princess Mary. There was feasting, jousts and a tour of Henry's favourite and most magnificent palaces, Richmond, Hampton Court and Windsor. Here they signed a new treaty – a defence pact against France – and the Princess Mary was formally betrothed to the emperor, just three years after her previous betrothal to the French Dauphin.

Henry was often generous with his gifts and his titles, but Arthur was not raised to the nobility until Charles Brandon had been created duke of Suffolk. Then Arthur could finally be created Viscount Lisle. His ceremony was conducted on 25 Apr 1523 where:

This order was kept and fulfilled in all points at Bridewell beside the Blackfriars at London at the creation of the worthy and valiant knight Sir Arthur Plantagenet, son Illegitime of the most famous prince King Edward the fourth; which was created Viscount Lisle, and was led by the Earl of Devon in his habit of estate on his right hand, and the Lord Roos in his parliament robes … his gown that master Garter had was of black velvet furred with martens.[12]

Later in the year, sea raids on French towns and a disastrous land campaign with a two-pronged attack led by the duke of Suffolk and the earl of Surrey turned into a disaster. For now the king's war was over. Arthur does not appear to have taken part in the fighting, instead he was commissioned to 'muster all dwellers on the seacoast'[13] to prepare for a possible French invasion.

On 8 May the following year he was made a knight of the garter and allocated the seventh stall on the prince's side in the chapel at Windsor. Arthur's coat of arms was royal, displaying the coat of King Edward IV quartered with Ulster and Mortimer under a bar sinister denoting an illegitimate birth. According to Brooke in Bank's book on dormant baronage, 'a bastard has no right to any arms but his father's chief coat, to show he was the natural son of such a man'.[14] Although Arthur had royal blood, he had a very humble background.

In 1524 Arthur was granted warden and keeper of the king's forest and park of Clarendon near Salisbury, although the king would later have reason to reprimand him for the decay of his deer and game and to tell him to have 'better respect' for them, or else 'you may be assured we shall discharge you of your office there'.[15] Arthur may have been kin and his elder but Henry would never shirk from telling him how to do his job properly.

In January 1525 Arthur was sent to take an inventory of stores at the king's beer houses in Portsmouth – beer was an important part of the provisions for sailors and upwards of 500 barrels a day were needed – and Henry VII had built three brewing houses there 'to serve his shippes at such tyme as they shaul go to the se in tyme of warre'.[16] Accompanying Arthur was Francis Bryan, with whom he would have a lasting friendship. Two new beer houses had been built in Portsmouth in 1513, making five to inventory: the 'Rose', the 'Lion', the 'Dragon', the 'White Hart' and the 'Anchor', to continue a steady supply during Henry VIII's reign.

Arthur was high in Henry's favour, even though they had the odd disagreement, and more appointments were to come. This was the king's heyday and he showed his gratitude to those that were loyal. In July 1525 Arthur was made vice-admiral on wages of around £100 a year. The king's son Henry Fitzroy was actually Lord High Admiral, but at 6 years old it was only a title and the role actually fell to Arthur who was responsible for overseeing the administration of the navy, from ship-building to combating piracy. On one occasion he wrote to Wolsey:

> I sent a balinger of mine with xx men in her to sea because of great robberies that were done upon the sea. And it fortuned my said ship and servants to recounter with a Spaniard … in a pink and xv men with him; and in the same recounter they slew ij of my men out of hand and sore hurt vj other of them; and my servants slew ix of them and vj took their boat and ran away…[17]

He ends the letter by telling him he has never been sicker in his life from a surfeit of eating fried stockfish!

In February 1525 Henry saw another chance to attack France when the French king was captured at the Battle of Pavia, but without funds and no support from Charles V, his plans came to nothing. Instead, negotiations started for a peace deal. Francis I's mother, Louise of Savoy, acting as regent for her son, negotiated with Cardinal Wolsey, and on 30 August 1525, the Treaty of the More, was signed between England and France. England would be at peace with her old enemy at least for a time.

Whereas Arthur would have had his work cut out for him with another war, he now had time for other things. While in London serving the king, he stayed at Blackfriars, but until his later purchase of a family manor, it appears that he either lived at Portchester or at Segenworth, one of the Wayte family homes. He had been granted the keepership of Portchester Castle, situated in Portsmouth harbour, and received an advance to build a storehouse and quay at the castle as well as to 'repair the timber work of the halls, kitchen chambers, towers, houses, and lodgings'[18] at his own cost. In 1526 Henry VIII spent six days with him so it must have been in lodgings suitable for a king, and Henry was impressed at the 'right great cheer'[19] he had with his uncle. We know he was also there in April and May of 1527 from signed receipts kept in his papers.

By 1525/6 Arthur had three daughters, Frances, Elizabeth and Bridget, but where his family were living is uncertain. They may have been with him at Portchester or perhaps more likely at Segenworth, closer to Titchfield. This property would not come into his possession until 1528, but he may have already been renting it as another receipt dating from August 1526 places him there. We lose sight of his wife around this time so it could be possible that she died giving birth to their last daughter. Elizabeth was buried at Titchfield Abbey but would later be reinterred at St Peter's Church after the abbey was dissolved and later turned into Place House, the home of Thomas Wriotheseley, 1st Earl of Southampton.

We don't know how much Arthur cared for his first wife, but the king was definitely fed up with his. Henry had realised that Katherine would never give him the heir he longed for. Searching for a reason why and looking for a way to end his marriage, Henry used the Bible as his excuse. Leviticus says: 'if a man shall take his brother's wife, it is an unclean thing he hath uncovered his brother's nakedness; they shall be childless'.[20] By Katherine being first married to his brother Arthur, Henry believed they had committed a sin and were being punished by God. Or that is the way he went about ridding himself of his queen, now he was enamoured of Anne Boleyn.

Anne was the daughter of Thomas Boleyn and Elizabeth Howard. Born at Blickling Hall and educated in France, she had returned home to become one of the queen's ladies-in-waiting. She had almost married James Butler, the 9th Earl of Ormond, and had been betrothed to Henry Percy, later Earl of Northumberland, but both relationships were quashed. Her older sister Mary had once been the king's mistress, but it was Anne who had now caught the king's eye.

Henry had ordered Wolsey to convene a secret ecclesiastical court to examine the validity of his marriage but he could not rule on such a matter and referred it to Rome. In fact, Henry's divorce from Katherine, his 'great matter', would continue for the next six years and he would look for support from his sometime-enemy, the French king, Francis.

In October 1527 Arthur had the honour of being sent to France with Sir Nicholas Carew and John Taylor, Master of the Rolls, to present the Order of the Garter to Francis I, 'so that these two Princes may henceforth wear one collar'.[21] Henry had already received the French equivalent of the Order of St Michael, and it was another move to cement the peace between them.

The crossing from Dover to Calais was rough and Arthur wrote to Wolsey of the delays but eventually they arrived in Paris. Taylor reported back to Wolsey:

My lord Lysley and College can plainlier declare unto your Grace than I the costly cheer and entertainment at the court. Thanks to God and St. George, all the ceremonies were done with d[ue] solemnities and honourable expedition of both parties ... The garter, the robe, and the collar became the King well; and as he took his horse, Madame looked out at a window to see the King and my lord Lysley ... The sight pleased her so well (she was moved to tears). In the delivery of the garter, my lord Lysley and Mr Carew have demeaned themselves according to their duty.[22]

The king was pleased with his uncle and at this stage had no reason to doubt his loyalty, or to deem him anything but a competent and dutiful servant.

Arthur was not wealthy but had certainly been rewarded over the years and was assessed for the subsidy on lands at £800 in 1527, the same as Sir Thomas Boleyn. His friends Sir Francis Bryan and Sir William Kingston were assessed at £400 and £280 respectively. In 1528 Arthur had enough funds to buy the manor at Soberton in Hampshire which would become his home. This purchase also included the manors of:

Segenworth, Chark, Lee, Sutton, West Stratton, medsted otherwise called Minsted, Bury, Alverstoke, and Soberton, with the appurtenances and all other lands, tenements, rents, reversions, successions, advowsons of churches, chapels, hospitals, villeins, warrens, woods, waters, mills, fishings, commons, leets, law-days, liberties, franchises, and hereditaments whatsoever.[23]

Arthur bought the lands for £2,000 from John Wayte, 'his kinsman', which shows his link to the Waytes as blood kin. Curiously, provision was made for John, for as well as payment he was to receive 'meat, drink, and lodgings within the house of the said Viscount at all times hereafter when the said John will come and be with the said Viscount during the life of the said John'.[24]

This John Wayte is referred to in a family will as 'John the Innocent', and in a later letter to Lady Lisle he is mentioned as follows: 'it shall stand well with my lord's honour to see somewhat to the fool'.[25] There is some suggestion that this land transaction was a little strange because of John's capabilities. In the same letter John can only be trusted with small sums of money so 'he should not spend all at one time'.[26] Arthur may not have paid the full amount to his kinsman and instead just provided for him, but until when we do not know. He would not live with Arthur when he moved to Calais and there would be no more correspondence concerning him.

By now Arthur owned various estates and land, although the Dudley lands from his first marriage returned to her family. He would be caught up for many years with their management albeit helped by the extremely competent Sir Anthony Windsor, Lisle's receiver-general, and he would soon be in charge of even more.

In 1529 Arthur married Honor Grenville, daughter of Sir Thomas Grenville, lord of the manors of Stowe in Kilkhampton, Cornwall and Bideford, Devon. Honor's father had been an esquire of the body to Henry VII and Sheriff of Cornwall. Although the Grenville family was a prominent one, it was of a lower status than Arthur's first wife. Honor was born around 1493 and had married Sir John Basset of Tehidy and Umberleigh in 1515. Basset was around thirty years older than her and already had three daughters from his first marriage. Honor would give him several more – Philippa, Katherine, Anne, Mary, and three sons, George, John and James. Basset died in 1538 leaving Honor the care of his daughters and a life interest in his properties, some of which would cause Honor legal battles for many years to come.

Apart from managing his burgeoning portfolio of property and land, Arthur was interested in trade and to this end he bought shares in the ship *Marie Cheriton*, originally built by John Cheriton, a merchant from Exeter, that would be renamed the *Mary Plantagenet*. In 1530 he bought the fourth and final share of the ship from Nicholas Lymet, an apothecary. Instead of a cash payment he negotiated with Lymet that he could send thirty tons of goods on each voyage until the value of £100 had been reached. We will find out more about Arthur's ship later, but for now he would charter it for others' use and the trading of goods such as salt, cloth, herrings, wine and woad. Lisle provided the crew of twenty-four men and two boys for one such charter, all under the captainship of John a Borough, an expert mariner.

In 1531 Pope Clement ruled that Henry was forbidden to remarry and if he did so, his children would be seen as illegitimate. Further he forbade 'any one in England, of ecclesiastical or secular dignity, universities, parliaments, courts of law, &c., to make any decision in an affair the judgment of which is reserved for the Holy See. The whole under pain of excommunication',[27] but Henry didn't care. On 11 February 1531 Henry VIII became Supreme Head of the Church in England and Wales, 'as far as the law of Christ allows'.[28] Like many others, Arthur and his wife held traditional religious views and it was a change that would send shockwaves across the country.

In the summer, the king and queen were at Windsor Castle when Henry decided enough was enough. Impatient to be with Anne, he left the castle taking his court with him, leaving Katherine behind with just her daughter and her servants. Henry would never see his wife again. From now on he would live openly with Anne and she was queen in all but name.

In September, she was created Marquis of Pembroke at a lavish ceremony at Windsor Castle. Now she was of high enough status to be introduced to the King of France, Francis I. Henry had arranged to meet with Francis with a select band of nobles, Arthur included. For all intents and purposes it was supposed to be a political meeting to discuss the threat posed by the Ottoman Empire, but in reality Henry wanted Francis' support for his divorce and subsequent remarriage.

Anne was to be accompanied by English ladies of the nobility but many made their excuses and refused to go. Arthur's wife Honor, however, was chosen to serve her and it meant she could travel with her husband to a place – although they did not know it yet – would become their home.

In October 1532 the king and his 2,000-strong entourage crossed the channel to Calais and were warmly welcomed by Lord Berners, the King's Deputy, who accompanied them to the Church of St Nicholas for a thanksgiving mass before showing them to their lodgings at the Exchequer, which had been especially refurbished for their visit. For the next ten days, they inspected Calais and its defences, went hawking, ate and drank well and enjoyed their time together. Although Anne had a suite of seven rooms, the king's and her bedchambers were connected and it was an open secret that they spent their evenings together.

Henry then rode out from Calais to meet Francis at Sandingfield Abbey (St Inglevert) and both of the royal entourages went on to Boulogne for four days of hunting and feasting. Anne was to have been greeted by a French lady of high birth, either Queen Eleanor (whom Francis had married six years after the death of Queen Claude) or the king's sister, but neither would agree to meet her and the four-day trip became a men-only sojourn. Instead of a formal reception, Anne was to meet Francis informally.

Anne stayed in Calais while Henry rode off with Arthur by his side to meet Francis. Honor stayed with her and her other ladies while they awaited the return of two kings. Francis returned to Calais with Henry and on Sunday 28 October, Honor found herself dancing with the French king.

> At night the French King supped with our King, and there was a great banqueting. And after supper there came in a masque, my Lady marquis of Pembroke, my lady mary, my lady Derby, my lady Fitzwalter, my lady Rochford, my Lady Lisley, and my Lady Wallop, gorgeously apparelled, with visors on their faces; and so came and took the French king by the hand, and other lords of France and danced a dance or two. And after that the King took off their visors, and they danced with gentlemen of France an hour after.[29]

Afterwards, Anne had a private discussion with Francis and the French party stayed in Calais at the Staple Inn for five days before taking their leave. Eager to go home, Arthur and Honor had to wait with Henry and his beloved until the weather improved. For days they had to amuse themselves until there was a chance to set sail.

On 1 November Arthur and Honor were invited to dine with Cromwell – a man who would feature significantly in their lives, not necessarily for the better, but at this stage they still had a civil relationship. With Wolsey's downfall and death in 1530, Thomas Cromwell would soon be in a position of power and influence. Cromwell had worked in Thomas Wolsey's household and risen to become the Cardinal's secretary. By the end of 1530 he had joined the Privy Council and began his career which would see him rise to become Henry's chief minister and the king's principal secretary at the end of 1534. Cromwell and Arthur would have a tumultuous relationship in the future but their early letters are courteous, with Lady Lisle even sending him a gift of cheeses for his help.

Honor thanked him for their 'good supper' on their return to England which had not been without its perils.

> I would know of your good return to England, and how you passed the perilous danger of the sea, for my lord and I were in so great peril, for lack of a good pilot and daylight, that we stood in great danger of our lives, and that causes me to be the more desirous to know how you escaped.[30]

Given that Cromwell would have been travelling with the king who sailed back to Dover, it's possible that Arthur and Honor sailed a different route and docked at Southampton, which was only around seventeen miles from their home at Soberton.

It is thought that Henry first slept with Anne on this trip. To the king and his beloved it was a huge success, and to others it showed that the king had every intention of making Anne his queen, but the whole thing seemed a little off. Queen Katherine was still alive and well and married to Henry. With Henry completely ignoring that fact, he secretly married Anne on 25 January 1533 at Whitehall Palace; 1533 would be a year of change for them all but especially for Arthur.

Chapter Three

To Calais 1533

Henry VIII, King of England, had married Anne Boleyn for love – or lust – but Katherine would always consider herself queen – as others did. It has been suggested that Arthur, now referred to as Lord Lisle, was part of the pro-Boleyn faction who brought Anne to power, but this was a difficult time for those who supported Katherine and wanted to stay in favour. On the surface Lisle had to accept Henry's choice, even if his loyalties lay with Katherine. To keep in the king's good books, Anne had to be recognised as queen and Lisle must have shown how loyal and willing he was to do the king's bidding because he was rewarded with the post of Lord Deputy of Calais in March 1533, following the death of John Bourchier, 2nd Baron Berners, the previous deputy.

John Bourchier, Lord Berners, had died on 19 March and was buried in the church of Our Lady, Calais, leaving the position vacant. Berners had had a long tenure from 1520 and had his work cut out for him trying to maintain the fortifications. He was constantly in debt from managing his household and entertaining visiting dignitaries – something Lisle would soon experience. As an aside, Berners spent his spare time translating works such as *Froissart's Chronicles*, *The Golden Book of Marcus Aurelius*, *The History of Arthur of Lytell Brytaine* (Brittany), and a romance *Huon of Bordeaux*.

Historians over the years have credited Lisle as being incompetent, lacking in the qualities needed for such a post, and unable to manage such a position. In Lisle's defence, he took on a role that was not going to be easy, for a town that had its own in-fighting, was in a ruinous state and – out of times of war – was a forgotten outpost that was severely underfunded and undersupplied. Lisle didn't come to this position for no reason, apart from the king's belief in him, he had been vice-admiral, a member of the Council and had been knighted. Henry trusted him to do the job to the best of his ability, and it was also a role that he could not turn down even if he wanted to.

Calais became an English possession when it was captured after an almost year-long siege by Edward III in 1437. Froissart's Chronicle wrote of how the king said to his marshals:

> Sirs, take these keys of the town and castle of Calais and go and assume possession of them. Take the knights who are there and make them prisoners or else put them on parole: they are gentlemen and I will trust them on their word. All other soldiers, who have been serving there for pay, are to leave the place just as they are and so is everyone else in the town, men, women and children, for I wish to repopulate Calais with pure-blooded English.[1]

When its French inhabitants left, their property and spoils were split among the English. English and Latin became the town's official languages and Calais would remain crown property until its loss in 1558. The town, as well as the surrounding area known as the Marches or the Pale, came under English jurisdiction and included Guisnes, Hammes and Oye. It covered around twenty square miles stretching from Escalles in the west, to just short of Gravelines in the east and down to the border before Ardres.

Calais was a rectangular limestone walled and moated town on the north coast of France that housed around 4,000 inhabitants. As a fortified town it was enclosed and protected by ramparts, watchtowers and a series of four gates – the lantern gate, the milk gate, the Boulogne gate and the water gate. The lantern gate with the inscription: 'Then shalle the Frenchman Calais winne, when iron and leade lyke corke shall swimme'[2] on the north wall led to the harbour and Rysbank Tower; to the west was the imposing castle of Calais and off centre to the east was the market place where the Staple Hall and Town Hall stood.

Calais itself was both a military and commercial centre, home to England's largest permanent fighting force, and had once been governed by the Company of Merchants of the Staple of England – otherwise known as the Staplers. The Staplers were one of the oldest merchant company's dating as far back as 1282. Primarily involved in the wool trade they had previously had their base in Bruges, Dordrecht and Antwerp. They relocated to Calais in 1347 and in 1466 signed their first act of retainer – an agreement between the crown and Staplers – which gave them control of the town and commerce and made them responsible for maintaining Calais and paying its retinue with the profits from the wool trade. But by 1528 Sir Robert Wingfield, Lord Deputy before Lord Berners between 1523–1526, was complaining to Cardinal Wolsey that the Staplers had no money, and by 1532 they were over £22,000 in debt to the crown. By March 1533 the Staple was suspended and Thomas Cromwell, the king's secretary, was charged with sorting it out. It would be one of many problems Lisle would have to face.

Lisle would be taking over a position that throughout Calais' history had been called captain, lieutenant or deputy, and joining a long line of men who had sought to bring order to this little part of England in France. Lisle's patent set out his wages of 2 shillings a day plus a bonus of 20 marks a year, £100 from the manors of Marke and Oye (in the Pale) and £104 'spyall' money. He was allowed his own retinue of thirty-one soldiers, a spear, two archers and twenty-eight other men. Although Lisle would govern the town during peacetime, Calais had often been used as a 'bridgehead for invasions',[3] most recently in 1513 for Henry's campaign against the French, and given the king's changing relationship with his sworn enemy, it had to be maintained in case any further hostilities broke out. Lisle's new role would be a difficult one.

Those in Calais were made aware that Lisle would soon be taking up his position. Sir Christopher Garneys, Knight Porter, on hearing the news wrote: 'there is no friend ye have this day living more gladder of the news than I am',[4] and told him that Lord Berners' old house would be prepared for his coming, but for him to send someone over to view his new residence and detail what was needed. Lisle duly sent over John Atkinson, his chaplain, to look things over and sent on his personal belongings in a balinger belonging to the family, the *Sunday of Porchester.* Atkinson, writing in June, mentioned that food and fuel were needed – something that would not only be a problem for Lisle, but all of Calais' inhabitants.

In May, Thomas Cranmer, Archbishop of Canterbury, had declared Henry and Katherine's marriage null and void and announced Henry and Anne's marriage valid. Henry had one more role for Lisle to undertake before he left England, and that was to serve as chief panter (to serve the new queen's bread) at Anne Boleyn's coronation on 1 June. Whether Lisle supported him or not, he would never go against his nephew's wishes. Honor, his wife, held much more traditional beliefs so if anyone felt uncomfortable with the situation it was her. Given she had served Anne the previous year in Calais she was probably also in attendance at her coronation, if not serving the queen, at least as an invited guest.

The Tudor chronicler, Edward Hall, wrote:

> On 1 June Queen Anne was brought from Westminster Hall to St Peter's Abbey in procession, with all the monks of Westminster going in rich copes of gold, with thirteen mitred abbots; and after them all the king's chapel in rich copes with four bishops and two mitred archbishops, and all the lords going in their parliament robes, and the crown borne before her by the duke of Suffolk, and her two sceptres by two earls, and she herself going under a rich canopy of cloth of gold, dressed in a kirtle of crimson velvet decorated with ermine, and a robe of purple velvet decorated with ermine over that, and a rich coronet with a cap of pearls and stones on her head … And so she was brought to St Peter's church at Westminster, and there set in her high royal seat, which was made on a high platform before the altar. And there she was anointed and crowned queen of England by the archbishop of Canterbury and the archbishop of York.[5]

Afterwards at a banquet in the Great Hall at Westminster, 'The Earl of Sussex was sewer, Earl of Essex carver, Earl of Derby cup bearer, Earl of Arundel butler, Viscount Lisle panter, and Lord Grey almoner.'[6]

At the beginning of June, while Lisle was preparing to make the move to Calais, his friend Sir Francis Bryan and the Duke of Norfolk who were on diplomatic duties abroad enjoyed his hospitality in his new home – a home he had not yet seen. They were accommodated by Lisle's servants and 'continually sent at every meal for beer and wine, both French wine and Gascon, whereupon I caused your yeoman of the cellar, Petley, to give attendance upon them at their commandment, both early and late, and so he doth right well'.[7] Bryan sent his thanks before they journeyed on and that short note would be the first extant letter in the *Lisle Letters* between the two of a correspondence that would last for seven years.

When Lisle arrived in Calais on 10 June, he found it in a state of disrepair, just a year after he accompanied the king and Anne Boleyn to meet the king of France. For that occasion, the town had been made ready for a royal visit masking what Lisle now saw in the clear light of day. Calais was no longer the 'chief jewel of the English crown' it once was. It had been made ready for the king prior to his French campaign of 1513 and some money was spent on refortifying the town, but throughout the period from 1521 to 1528 several complaints about the state of the place had made their way to the Council, including one from Cardinal Wolsey who told them it was 'in no little disorder'.[8] Henry had seen for himself how bad things had become when he and Anne visited in 1532 and he drew up 'a devyse ... for the fortificacion of the saide towne',[9] that included his plans to improve the town's and harbour's defences – but none of the work had been carried out.

Regardless of the state of Calais, Lisle had to make it his home. Lisle, Honor and five of their children – Lisle's Frances and Honor's Philippa, Katherine, Mary and Anne – plus their household of between fifty and seventy servants, lived in Lord Berner's former home on the south side of Calais. Honor's two youngest daughters would go on to live with noble French families, leaving three young girls in the household. The rest of their family stayed in England. Lisle's daughter Elizabeth lived with her half-brother Sir John Dudley, and Bridget, his youngest daughter, was schooled at St Mary's Abbey in Winchester under the care of Dame Elizabeth Shelley, the abbess.

Their new home in Calais must have been a sizeable property with a large garden, big enough for the previous Lord Deputy to raise pheasants in, and Lisle continued to employ his gardener. People were especially proud of their gardens in Calais and one of its residents, Sir Robert Wingfield, had even managed to grow almonds, which he sent to the queen.

Lisle headed the Council of Calais as deputy. In the *Chronicle of Calais* in a list dated 1533, he was followed by Sir William Sandys, the Lieutenant of Guisnes, Sir Richard Grenville, the High Marshal, Sir John Wallop, the Lieutenant of the Castle of Calais, Sir George Carew, Lieutenant of Rysbank, Sir Edward Ryngeley, the Comptroller, Sir Thomas Palmer, Knight Porter, Lieutenants of Newnhambridge and Hammes, and William Sympson. the Vice Marshal. It is possible, however, that this list has been misdated as Carew and Palmer did not take up their positions until later. There were also other men in Calais that held sway, such as Sir Robert Wingfield and Sir Richard Whethill especially, who would not make life easy for the king's uncle.

But for now Lisle was held in esteem and many people started what would become a huge volume of correspondence full of news, requests for favours and appeals for appointments. Honor too kept up her own correspondence and answered others on her husband's behalf. She never wrote her own letters however, but dictated them. It is possible that she could not write, or just preferred to speak aloud while a secretary penned her missives. Unlike Lisle she had never learnt French or Latin.

Lisle kept in touch with men like Sir William Kingston who, way back in 1510, had ventured into exporting woollen cloth with him; Sir William Sandys, who was Lieutenant of Guisnes but was based in England as he was also Henry VIII's Lord Chamberlain; and Sir John Russell, the Earl of Bedford, comptroller of Henry's household, as well as his friends Sir Francis Bryan; Sir William Fitzwilliam, previous Captain of Guisnes between 1523–26; and Sir Henry Norris, who would later be executed for his supposed involvement with Anne Boleyn. At the time they were all prominent men at the Tudor court, had the king's ear and supported Lisle, and would try to help with his situation over the years. One of the saddest early letters he received was from Mary Tudor, the king's sister and Lisle's niece, who wrote with a shaky hand what must have been one of her last letters at the end of March, looking for a room in the garrison for a John Williams. She died three months later on 25 June at her home of Westhorpe Hall in Suffolk.

Lisle's first letter from Cromwell also touched on the favour of an appointment and asked that Bartholomew Petres, then employed as surgeon of Calais, was given his room in the retinue. He also alluded to a letter Lisle had previously sent him – not extant – that outlined some early problems in maintaining Calais, and Cromwell reassured him he would do his best 'to reduce and bring the same to such good pass and effect as shall be thought most requisite and expedient'.[10] It would be an empty promise.

We have seen that Calais' defences and fortifications were a major problem, but this was compounded by issues with the garrison or retinue and the problem of revictualling. The retinue consisted of 382 waged soldiers in 1535, plus 308 serving under them as private servants. On average, in peacetime, there were around 700 men in the garrison. At times of war the number swelled into the thousands. It has been estimated that it cost the crown £8,000 a year to keep the retinue, but wages were frequently late or unpaid and in past times the soldiers had mutinied against their conditions. Many of the men took to finding other forms of income and also worked in the town. As soldiers, or 'spears', their duties included keeping watch, going on patrol, monitoring the movements of any strangers, and the opening and closing of the four gates which was done with some ceremony. Starting in the morning, forty of the watch would accompany the porters to the deputy's house to retrieve the keys and to the tune of fife and drum, march to each gate to open it. They were closed an hour before noon to allow for dinner time and at night before the keys were returned to the deputy for safe-keeping to be 'locked in a coffer, which coffer always standeth by the deputy's bedside'.[11]

There were three regular groups of watches; the scout-watch, the search-watch and the stand-watch. If a member of the stand-watch was found asleep for the third time on his watch, his punishment was to be hoisted in a basket over the ramparts with bread, water and a knife. His only way out was to cut the rope and be unceremoniously dumped in the moat from a height of around 10ft.

In such a small town, one would think that during peacetime the running of the garrison would have been a relatively easy role, but the trouble for Lisle came with the granting of rooms, and therefore positions, given to men who wanted to join the retinue at Calais. It was a sought-after position with the promise of military experience, wages, and the honour of serving the king. By the terms of Lisle's patent he was:

> freely to expel his will and to discharge and remove from offices and rooms all and singular the aforesaid men called Souldeours and other horsemen, officers and ministers, and to appoint and swear-in others in their rooms and offices at his discretion, whensoever and wheresoever it shall seem expedient to the said Viscount Lisle for the good security or better safe-keeping and government of the aforesaid town and marches.[12]

But Henry VIII liked to give out rooms and offices as gifts or rewards, circumventing Lisle's authority. For instance, when the king granted Richard Blount a spears room, he was not rightly the next in line for such a position. Lisle wrote to Cromwell, 'notwithstanding I have the gift of all the spears in my patent and all other of the Retinue, yet the King's

Grace's pleasure and your desire shall be ever fulfilled in me'.[13] He had to obey his king, but the giving of rooms without due recourse to those who were waiting for their turn would cause many problems, as we shall see.

In a letter to the king from Lisle and the Council of Calais on 21 June, they write that 'the necessities of the town are many and great for lack of the ancient liberties which the town has always enjoyed, and they require quick remedy'.[14] Most supplies – food and fuel – were shipped from England to Calais, although some local produce was available. The arable land of the Pale was farmed for Calais inhabitants by a mix of nationalities, mostly French and Flemish, who produced mainly grain. There was also a lack of clothing and building materials. In 1521 Sir Robert Wingfield told Wolsey how badly Calais was being supplied, and in 1522 Berners and the Council sent a letter to the king to inform him how desperately Calais needed wood and fuel. Shortages were even further depleted when visiting dignitaries were accommodated, as in 1527 when Wolsey's entourage severely reduced their stocks. Prior to Lisle becoming deputy there had been some attempt to make Calais self-sufficient, but it had failed and by 1533 the shortages were at crisis level.

One trade that still thrived was in herrings. Herring season lasted from 29 September to 30 November and meant that around 300 foreign ships piled into the harbour to sell their wares in the market place. There would be more traders in the town and the watches increased. The banner-watch was responsible for maintaining order and a nightly report was taken to Lisle of the number of herring boats present and how many traders and sailors were on them.

So Lisle took on a position that saw him smack bang in the middle of several issues to deal with. Whether he knew quite how bad the situation was before he arrived in Calais is not clear. He did seem to have a hint of trepidation at this massive undertaking, but he hit the ground running and immediately began to build relationships with key people.

As if his work problems were not enough, Lisle also had ongoing personal problems, mostly to do with property. He held a vast portfolio in England and when he departed for Calais, people he trusted – such as William Seller at Soberton – were left to manage his estates and collect rents. One of the biggest disputes in which he was involved concerned the lands that had been left to his stepson from his first marriage, John Dudley. On the death of Lisle's first wife Elizabeth Grey, Dudley inherited all his father's property. Lisle had a life-long interest in these but Dudley had decided to sell the rights to his estates to several men, including Thomas Cromwell, William Popley, the Marquis of Exeter, and Edward Seymour, later to be Lord High Treasurer and, in Edward VI's reign, Lord Protector.

The dispute between Lisle and Seymour was drawn out and complicated, but Lisle had made an agreement with Seymour that meant he would get paid a yearly rent of £140 for his interest in the Somerset properties. Lisle also had control of the tenants, leases and feudal dues on the estate and naturally, with Seymour buying the rights to the land and receiving no profit from the estate, he wasn't happy with the deal. He offered Lisle £500 to release his interest but Lisle refused and would later take Seymour to court.

An historian has quoted Lisle as being 'extravagant, weak-willed and incapable',[15] and has suggested that Lisle gave out bribes so that this land dispute would go in his favour, which was really only getting started at this time and would continue for the next two years. But Lisle must have believed in his right to the lands in Somerset, and moreover he wasn't in England to sort out his own problems. He was stuck in Calais and had to negotiate with other people – his agents, his lawyers and his supporters at court – to do the work for him.

One man that would constantly support him over the years was his friend Sir Francis Bryan. Bryan wrote to him in July that he hoped to be heading home from his diplomatic duties in a month's time, 'against which time I, Sir Fras. Bryan, desire you to make more ready for me a soft bed than an hard harlot'.[16]

Sir Francis had a name for himself as a womaniser and it seems that perhaps in their younger days, Lisle may have been too as in his next letter Bryan jokes about their 'misliving':

Sir, whereas in your last letter I perceive that in Calais ye have sufficient of courtesans to furnish and accomplish my desires, I do thank you of your good provision. But this shall be to advertise you that since my coming hither I have called to my remembrance the misliving that ye and such other hath brought me to; for the which being repented, have had absolution of the Pope. And because ye be my friend, I would advertise you in likewise to be sorry of that ye have done, and ask my Lady your wife forgiveness, and, that forgiveness obtained, to come in all diligence hither to be absolved of the Pope.[17]

It may have all been tongue in cheek – something to provide light relief from the daily grind, and Lisle no doubt welcomed Bryan and enjoyed his company and friendly ear when he arrived on his way back to England, but entertaining would prove a costly business and contribute to the Lord Deputy's slow slide into debt.

Lisle had been surveying the town and, faced with fortifications in ruin, ordnance and artillery in decay and defences that were sorely in need of repair, he compiled a list with the Council and aldermen of Calais proposing what could be done. It included entries such as:

Becham tower. Two doors are to be new made in the lowest vault. The tower is somewhat too high and weak to bear ordnance on the top. The highest floor under the leads needs repair. The mount of the tower should be newly made or repaired.

The tower at Our Lady of the Wall. A door by the ground is to be repaired, with the vault over it. The tower is cloven in the top. There lacks a door at the leads.

Dublyn tower. Is very weak, never a good floor in it, and the walls are scarce able to bear a floor.[18]

The list goes on, with floors needing repair or replacing, doors lacking, leads and tiles missing and bulwarks to be mended, and is followed by a list of ordnance that would be needed to defend the town. Henry knew Calais was in no fit state, but at the time it was also not a priority. It was reasonably safe for the time being with neither the French king, Francis I nor Charles V, Holy Roman Emperor, interested in attempting to seize it for themselves.

Lisle also knew he needed to do something about bringing supplies into the town and he entered into an agreement with Henry Bourchier, the 2nd Earl of Essex. Essex could provide him with oxen, sheep and wood, and in return Lisle could send over wine and barrels of herring, sturgeon, cod and salmon, among other things. But even with this mutual agreement there were problems. The searcher or customs officer of Colchester, one Debnam, who despite being shown papers from both Essex and Lisle, was delaying transportation of the goods 'to the great disappointing of the victualling of the King's said town'.[19]

Essex wrote to Cromwell to complain and the situation rumbled on. Letters and Papers dates some of the correspondence to 1534, so it looks like Debnam was still obstructing the transport of goods. Lisle informed Cromwell that Debnam had seized oxen and not only that, but the searcher was swearing that:

> Lisle had ordered those who brought wine, herring, and other goods from Calais to England and back that they should neither pay custom nor allow customer, searcher or other of the King's officers to meddle with them.[20]

This was treasonous talk and Lisle's solicitor, Leonard Smyth, who heard Debnam casting aspersions on his master told him to watch what he said. Lisle hoped that Cromwell would certify the truth of his report and do something about the corrupt searcher. Debnam, at Cromwell's order:

> gave Smyth 10 marks for 10 oxen, but they were bought from the Earl of Essex for 20 marks, so that, including the charges of the ship and his servants, Lisle has lost 20l. and more.[21]

Lisle received a response from Ralph Sadler, Cromwell's secretary, who assured him that he would soon receive a warrant from the king for the victualling and also restitution for the missing and spoiled goods. Debnam would also be punished.

As Lisle's problems mounted, his nephew seemed unbothered at best, but Henry had a lot on his plate. In July he was excommunicated by Pope Clement VII, and the long awaited birth of his heir in September was a disappointment when Anne Boleyn gave birth to Princess Elizabeth, the future Elizabeth I of England, at the Palace of Placentia (Greenwich). He is reported to have said 'You and I are both young, and by God's grace, boys will follow....'[22] His mood was often sour as it must have been when Cromwell had broached him about Lisle's problems. A more cheerful member of the royal family who visited Lisle in Calais around this time was Henry's illegitimate son, Henry Fitzroy, the Duke of Richmond, who accompanied the Duke of Norfolk to meet with the French king.

Lisle and the Council had written to Cromwell several times about the situation in Calais and received either no reply or replies that did nothing to help. They had considered other ways to retain the use of corn for the benefit of Calais' inhabitants but Cromwell's next letter basically told him, by the king's command, not to meddle.

I ensure your lordship the King's Highness is not a little displeased with that your desire, but supposeth your business to be very small that will in any wise importune his Highness with any such matters, saying that before this time the town and marches of Calais hath been well maintained, and prospered without any such new devices.[23]

This was obviously untrue. Calais had been struggling for a long time as previous Lord Deputy's had pointed out. But Cromwell was not done, he also mentioned Honor.

For although my lady be right honourable and wise, yet in such causes as longeth to your authority her advice and discretion can little prevail.[24]

It is not clear what Honor had done to attract Cromwell's disdain but it would also not be the last time he wrote to Lisle of his wife's actions. The letter ended with the stinging rebuke: 'I pray your Lordship to consider the same, and to importune the King's Highness with none other matters than of necessity ye ought to.'[25] Cromwell would always stand between Lisle and his nephew, making Lisle's future problems all the more difficult.

But as well as corresponding with Cromwell and acquaintances in England and dealing with his fellow Calisiens and those living in the Pale, Lisle had to make new relationships with French officials.

Oudart du Biez, the Seneschal of Boulogne, who Lisle had met in 1527 when he presented the Garter to the king of France, was one of the first to welcome him and hoped they would make 'good cheer' together. They would maintain a cordial relationship throughout Lisle's tenure, and in October Biez wrote to Lisle about a young boy in trouble. He had been informed that he was:

At your town of Calais in the lodging of Pere Brisselet, where I am told he hath been for some time. And because the poor youth hath no money to defray his expenses, he hath been kept prisoner these six or seven months. Where he remaineth yet in great poverty, and as it appeareth, must so continue, because neither the youth nor his mother can pay that which is demanded of him. Wherefore, my Lord Deputy, I pray you in favour to me to have the poor child recommended to you, for it is great pity thus to maltreat a child of such age as he is of, and also it is not reasonable.26

We can only hope that Lisle found a way to help him. The edited *Lisle Letters* only contain seven letters from Biez but there are in fact fifty-eight in the original papers; as one historian points out, 'St Clare Byrne was largely uninterested in this correspondence',27 but it proves that Lisle built and maintained these relationships with his French counterparts throughout his tenure.

Another man he maintained a relationship with was John Cheriton from whom he had bought his ship the *Mary Plantagenet*. Cheriton was a merchant and acted as Lisle's agent on several sea voyages. It is obvious that their relationship was an old one from the end of a letter he sent to Lisle in September from Pisa where he wished him and Honor 'wholesome air for your health as your Lordship had at Porchester Castle and at Soberton'.28 This letter written in Pisa also contained the news that on Lisle's instructions he had sold the ship to one Antonio di Marini, a man he did not trust, still carrying ordnance from Porchester Castle at the time. Cheriton would stay with the ship and at the time was sailing the Mediterranean trade route, but he would not prove to be the most lucky mariner and his further letters will detail the troubles he found himself in.

Lisle's relationships with the well-established citizens of Calais did not get off to a good start. In-fighting in the town would constantly raise its head. A small incident now occurred that was ballooned out of proportion. Christopher Garneys, Knight Porter, (who we met previously when he wrote to welcome Lisle to Calais) was in a spot of bother. During herring time the volume of traffic in and out of the gates increased and when the gate became blocked with carts and wagons, the Yeoman Porters tried to break up the carters and clear the jam. Apparently after much back and forth they sent for Garneys, who saw that one carter in particular was causing the problem. In his own words: 'I strake him between the neck and the shoulders with the little staff I bear in my hand for his lewd words and for correction in ensample of other like rude persons.'[29] Both Garneys, in a letter to Cromwell, and Lisle in his letters to the Duke of Norfolk and Cromwell to explain the situation, pointed out that this was typical behaviour – other officers had done the same in the past to regain order – even though technically striking another man was a criminal offence.

Garneys recalled what happened next:

Whereupon one in this town whom I took for my special friend sent for the carter to his house and asked him if I had stricken him at the gate, who said Yea; and then he said he would cause him to have a bill of complaint made and warranted him to have a great amends, and willed him to put it up to my Lord Deputy against me.[30]

This man – the carter's special friend – was Sir Edward Ryngeley, a member of the Council of Calais who was not averse to causing trouble. Sick and tired of Calais, Ryngeley had made a situation that Lisle could have easily dealt with into a much more serious matter. Not only did he help the carter to raise a complaint, it was one that made its way to England and the King's Council. Cromwell, however, was supportive of what Lisle called 'a correction rather than a debat [brawl]'.[31] He wrote that after debate by the Council they had decided, for once in agreement with Lisle, that:

the said stroke was given but only for correction and for none intent to break the law, statute, or ordinance of Calais, do think the same but a very light matter to make any such business of and no cause why the said Sir Christopher should be put to any molestation for the same. Wherefore your lordship may let it pass, and weigh it as it is.[32]

Something Lisle would have done anyway without Ryngeley's interference. It was such a small matter taken out of proportion when he had so much worse to deal with.

Towards the end of the year, Lisle had been trying his best to get Calais re-victualled before the winter. As a matter of good form he wrote to tell Cromwell that he had arranged for corn to be brought in from all parts of the Pale, 'so that we are now, thanked be God, ... meetly well stored of wheat'.[33] He also hoped that cattle would be brought in and it must have been a relief for him to know that the town would be provided for.

Cromwell was not so supportive this time and was unimpressed by Lisle taking the initiative, replying that, 'I assure your lordship ye do not well, in causing people to bring in their goods and other things which needeth not.' Lisle was told to look to the defence and fortifications of the town and moreover that, 'it is thought to the King's Highness and his council here that your practices and doings in it be very ill and not well nor circumspectly considered'.[34]

As you can imagine Lisle was obviously angered and responded that if Henry truly knew what was going on, that would not have been his reaction. He reminded Cromwell that by the king's order he was in charge of Calais and that himself and the Council had done what was necessary to make provision for Calais, 'which hath been long in necessity for lack of victual out of England'. He ended by saying that when the king found out the truth of the matter that Cromwell's comments 'shall be clearly wiped out, or else [Lisle] would be very sorry'.[35]

When he didn't hear back he wrote again. We don't have Cromwell's reply but by 16 December something had happened because Lisle was writing to him that he knew he had approached the king to remedy their situation. However, he had also heard rumours that people around the king were telling him that 'three score thousand quarters of wheat'[36] had been shipped to Calais, and he denied that they had received any such supplies telling Cromwell to have the customs books checked.

Lisle had also asked his friend Sir Francis Bryan to push the king to see goods were shipped over to them for the winter when he visited him at Calais on his way back from a diplomatic mission to Marseilles to visit the French king and gain his support for Henry's divorce. Lisle warmly welcomed his old acquaintance and when he left Bryan told Lady Lisle that her little dog Purquoy (from the French 'pourquoi', meaning why) would be an excellent gift for Queen Anne, although Honor was loathe to part with it.

Lisle was still concerned with the lack of fuel for the winter and that if it was not remedied, was scared 'this town doth and shall suffer more than it may goodly bear',[37] but soon some provisions began to come in. A warrant for Lisle's household by order of the king permitted the export to Calais of sixty beefs, 300 muttons, sixty lambs, twenty porks as well as stocks of fish, butter, cheese and tallow.

At the end of December Lady Lisle received a letter from John Husee to tell her he had arrived safely at Dover and was about her business – her ribbons would be sent before New Year – this short note dealing with something so trivial heralds in someone that would be crucial to the Lisles, and someone who would deal with every aspect of their lives as their most trusted agent, contributing around 500 pieces of correspondence to the *Lisle Letters*. Husee would be their ear to the ground, so likeable that people easily talked to him and passed on information. He would be invaluable to Lisle – not only as his man of business but as an adviser and a counsellor – something Lisle would sorely need in the years to come.

Chapter Four

Life as Lord Deputy
1534

Husee took to his role as Lisle's agent with gusto, dealing not only with the court and Lisle's interests, but also Honor's needs and her interests in her family lands. He started the year by writing to Lisle that his new year's gift to the king of £20 in gold was well received. He had presented it in person and was delighted the king had accepted it 'right lovingly'.

Sir Francis Bryan had been at court and he wrote also to tell his friend and Honor that he had given Queen Anne her little dog. Honor loved animals and kept several, never wanting to part with any of them, but Bryan assured her that Anne was delighted with Purquoy that 'was so proper and so well liked by the Queen that it remained not above an hour in my hands but that her Grace took it from me'.[1]

Lisle was starting to feel he should never have left court. He was doing his best with Calais but by being across the water, he was far from the king's ear and trusted men like Bryan and Norris were needed to speak to him on his behalf. John Rokewood was a spear and member of the Calais Council who had returned to England for a time and took up Husee's role (who had returned to Calais for a time) as a major correspondent of court news. If Lisle was feeling left out and wondering what was said about him at court, Rokewood tried to reassure him by telling him that the king thought him 'the most meetest and best'[2] for the job.

This year Sir Thomas Palmer, Captain of Newnham Bridge, would take up his role as Knight Porter of Calais. He was granted the reversion of the office in 1526 but Sir Christopher Garneys, who had so warmly welcomed Lisle to Calais, still held the position until his death in October when Sir Thomas Palmer took over the vacancy. In a letter to Cromwell which is extremely chatty he seems to be outlining his character as worthy of the position he would come into. He makes the point that Garneys received many stipends but here he was '500 marks in debt and never a groat in my purse', and proceeded to explain at length why he was so poor, including that he was:

> put in garrison at Guisnes, and within a year was taken prisoner, and lost 7 of mine own horse that were taken with me, and paid £100 for my ransom, without help of any man living of a groat, and was compelled to buy 7 other great horses or else lose my wages.

He must have been worried about people maligning his character as he assures Cromwell all that he writes is 'neither lie nor fable', and adds the dramatic flourish to have pity on him and 'not suffer me to die till I be sick'.[3] He introduces himself to Lisle in January, although they may have met before when he was one of Henry's gentlemen ushers.

The issue with Edward Seymour over John Dudley's lands would rumble on this year. Seymour told Lisle that he should have none of the lands, and he wanted 'three score pounds … which of right I ought to have',[4] but he was content to have two judges decide on the matter. There was even more trouble over land in Calais. Sir Robert Wingfield, mayor of Calais, had been granted marsh land known as the Main Brook but would be more commonly referred to as Wingfield's Marsh, that covered around 1,000 acres. He had drained the land but it acted as a natural defence and the Council, Lisle included, was concerned it left Calais open to attack and looked to the king for his help in the matter. Wingfield had a long history in the town. He was joint marshal from 1513 to 1519, lieutenant of the castle from 1523 to 1526, and had served as deputy from 1526 to 1531. He was not going to give up his land easily nor go down without a fight.

In every effort to make sure the town was victualled, Lisle kept up his pressure on Cromwell. They had received goods the previous year but it was an ongoing problem, as were the defences that needed rebuilding, and he was once again asking for money for the building and repairing of such works. There seems some urgency for this request with rumours that Charles V, Holy Roman Emperor, might have been considering hostilities with England but as Rokewood informed him, there was no bruit or rumour of war at court at present. Even so, he felt that the king would make sure the town was victualled and money found for the fortifications just in case. Lisle was aware that if the political situation changed he might be called upon to fight and to that end he had asked his nephew to provide him with a suit of armour. There was some delay in receiving it as Henry wanted to pick it out himself; being of the same stature, only the king's would fit Lisle.

Rokewood also informed him of a rumour he had heard that Lisle was to lose Porchester Castle and the Forest of Bere. On hearing this snippet of information he rushed to find Norris and Bryan, men he could trust to take Lisle's side and was reassured that the rumour was not true. Henry had no plans to take anything from him, they said, but only to increase his gifts to his uncle – which sounds much like the king trying to appease Lisle temporarily. It was yet another reason for Lisle to wish he was at court and able to fight his own battles.

In March Lisle heard from Thomas Percy, master of his ship, the *Sunday of Porchester*. He recounted a trip that was probably made the previous year when they encountered piracy and perhaps indulged a little in it themselves on their way to Ireland. The ship the *Trinity George* of Plymouth had taken two guns and three chambers from a Breton ship, and in turn the crew of the *Sunday*, captained by a William Fisher, had relieved them of their spoils. However, on the request of Thomas Sayer, part owner of the *Trinity George*, it was Thomas Percy who was arrested when he stopped at Plymouth. Percy wrote to Lisle to ask him to call Fisher before him for the truth of the matter. Obviously he felt he had taken the blame for something that the ship's captain had ordered his men to do. Thomas Sayer, believing the Breton ship to be 'a pirate and robber on the sea', lay claim to the guns and chambers and sought compensation from Percy. Now Percy was asking Lisle for the money back because as well as his financial loss he had also suffered 'punishment of his body'.[5] As with a lot of Lisle's correspondence, we don't know the outcome, but given there are no other letters from Percy it is likely that the situation was settled to his liking.

Lisle heard from Cheriton throughout the year and he seems to have been one of the most unlucky mariners of his time! In February he had been at Bordeaux licking his wounds after losing his entire cargo of silks, cotton, alum, woad and mastic when the Portuguese ship carrying it sank. The ordnance destined to be delivered to England for the king was still in Italy. He had arrived back in England eventually with a cargo of wine but feared this would be taken from him against his losses and the goods due to his buyers. He appealed to Lisle for his help 'to restrain again all my enemies'.

Lisle had to keep abreast of naval matters. After all, he had been vice-admiral, had his own ships and managed a sea port, so it was important to him to keep up with maritime news. He heard that three men, Richard Swift, John Buck and George Shaa or Shaw – all currently employed in Calais – had taken to piracy. More commonly referred to as Swift, Buck and George, George was one of Lisle's servants who had come with him from Soberton. The three men had high hopes for a swashbuckling life on the sea and Lisle, completely ignorant of their plans, had given them licence to travel to England where:

> They minded to get a ship or two more, and good fellows to the number of two or three hundred tall men, and then they would keep the seas in two parties and go over to the Cape and the Isles of Surreye whereas they purposed to obtain great many booties.[6]

There were rich pickings to be had in the Channel from boats of all nationalities and a ready market in Ireland where they could sell the spoils. But their life on the high sea barely got underway. A man they had tried to encourage to join them, Michael James of Hampton, informed John Cooke, the commissary of the Admiralty, of their intentions and he was now hot on their trail. As they lay in wait for two Breton ships near Yarmouth, they were boarded by real pirates who wanted to borrow their 'litill cokk' (a small boat) to row to the Isle of Wight to sell some sailcloth in exchange for victuals. The two men who were sent ashore, Peryn and Webbe, were arrested by Cooke, as were Buck and George. Swift evaded capture for the time being but the real pirates, who had 'a sword and buckler, and 3 of them were in velvet doublets and guarded hoses, cut, and with sarcanet under', spent the night in a beerhouse in Ryde and unfortunately '6 men drowned, that hath been thrown overboard by these pirates, and some of them hath had stones tied about their necks'.[7] These men – around eighty of them – were the real deal, whereas Swift, Buck and George had never really got started, their dreams of loot and life on the high sea dashed.

A man that appears now in the correspondence for the first time is Thomas Cranmer, Archbishop of Canterbury and supporter of the

English reformation. Although he would feature in the coming years, and especially around matters of religion, for now he was asking Lisle to look into the case of a widow of Calais, Elizabeth Beston, who complained she had suffered injury from one William Berdiseley, pertaining to a will. While Lisle was asked to administer justice in the case as he saw fit, he could only marvel at the news that was next sent to him of a woman, Alice Wolfe, who had made a daring escape from the Tower of London and would suffer a pirate's death.

Eight months earlier Alice had helped her husband John (who had also been implicated in the case of 366 missing crowns) and three other men, John Westall, Robert Garrard and John Litchfield, murder two foreign merchants. Alice had kept the two Italian merchants, Jerome de George and Charles Benche, pleasantly occupied at a house until nightfall when she and Westall led them to a boat, ostensibly to return them to their lodgings. Garrard and Litchfield waited, posing as watermen while John Wolfe lay hidden in the stern. Once they were out on the river, Wolfe jumped out of his hiding place and stabbed Charles Benche several times, fatally wounding him. Jerome de George was attacked by all four men and his neck broken. After stripping their bodies of money, jewels, keys and rings, they placed them face-to-face, wrapped in chains and weighed down with stones and threw them in the river. Back on land the culprits made their way to the merchant's lodgings and stole possessions from their chambers to the tune of £100.

They were confined to the Tower where Alice swiftly made friends, apparently using her feminine wiles, to try to escape her fate. Because the murder had occurred on the River Thames, they would face a pirate's death by being hung in chains over the river at low water so the rising tide would drown them – a particularly gruesome way to go.

William Denys, a servant of the Lieutenant of the Tower, showed her a way to escape from her gaol in Coldharbour Tower but when he was found talking to her, he was dismissed. Another servant, Bawde – who would later claim that he was in love with Alice, helped her to escape. Alice and Bawde had struck up a friendship when her husband had previously spent time in the Tower, and in him she found an ally.

John Grenville writing to Lisle told him the details of the escape. Bawde had:

With counterfeit keys opened the prison door where Wolfe his wife was, and conveyed her out of the Tower with two ropes tied to the embattlements: and after he had conveyed her down, went down himself to her and so together until they came to the Tower Hill or thereabouts.[8]

But here they were stopped by watchmen who became suspicious seeing Alice dressed like a man and they were returned to the Tower. Not only did Alice and her husband endure the fate she tried so hard to escape, but Bawde was confined to the 'Little Ease' – a tiny cell so small it was not possible to either sit or stand – racked and hanged, all for his love of Alice.

Lisle had to rely on other people for news like this of what was happening in England. News such as when Sir Brian Tuke informed him that Queen Katherine was now called the Princess Dowager of Wales, or when Thomas Palmer told him he was unable to speak with Norris to further Lisle's suits as he was 'ridden to my Lady Princess',[9] and there were sometimes vital pieces of information missing, it being too dangerous to consign details to paper. He had, in fact, escorted Lady Mary, along with the Duke of Norfolk and Sir William Fitzwilliam, to Princess Elizabeth's new household at Hatfield and as Chapuys put it, it was no trip to the countryside, but 'the Princess, who refused to accompany the Bastard on her removal to another house, was put by force by certain gentlemen into a litter with the aunt of the King's mistress'.[10] The changes wrought by Henry marrying Anne Boleyn would continue to have repercussions.

Husee had been in Calais but was soon to return to England where he often stayed at the Red Lion Inn in Southwark. Lisle missed his direct link to Cromwell as Husee would patiently wait to talk to the man who would soon be confirmed as the king's principal secretary and try to get instant answers for his master. As soon as Husee was back in England he delivered Lisle's letters to Cromwell, but he warned Lisle to keep his latest report to himself saying: 'there are some there which awaiteth to take your lordship in snare … I trust they shall be knowen, as well as some others here, which beareth your lordship fair face and a double dissimuling heart.'[11] It would not be the first time Husee had to warn his master of those who wished him harm and it shows that Lisle trusted people too easily. He wasn't as politically astute as the other nobles at court – a place of continuous movement and machinations – and in Calais he was far removed from those who had the king's ear and spoke against him.

While Lisle was busy with issues like rumours of the king coming to Calais, or Cromwell telling John Benolt, secretary of Calais, that he marvelled why the retinue had not been paid their wages, there were major changes happening in England. In March the first Act of Succession was passed by parliament that secured the succession on the children of Henry VIII and Anne Boleyn, meaning Lady Mary was declared a bastard and Elizabeth and any other heirs of this marriage would inherit the crown. People were required to swear an oath and those that refused were subject to a charge of treason under the Treasons Act 1534 which stated:

> If any person or persons, after the first day of February next coming, do maliciously wish, will or desire, by words or writing, or by craft imagine, invent, practise, or attempt any bodily harm to be done or committed to the king's most royal person, the queen's, or their heirs apparent, or to deprive them or any of them of their dignity, title, or name of their royal estates … That then every such person and persons so offending … shall have and suffer such pains of death and other penalties, as is limited and accustomed in cases of high treason.[12]

Lisle first heard of Stephen Gardiner's, the Bishop of Winchester, refusal to swear the oath from Thomas Palmer. Gardiner had previously been Wolsey's secretary and in 1529 became the king's. Although not directly stated he mentions that he 'is out of the Secretaryship'[13] and this is when Cromwell officially took over the position. Queen Katherine and the Princess Mary also refused to sign the oath and Katherine was banished to Kimbolton Castle near Huntingdon. Two other major characters in Tudor history, Thomas More and John Fisher, also refused to swear to the oath. More claimed he could not agree to 'the spiritual validity of the king's second marriage',[14] and he refused to accept that the king's marriage to Katherine was annulled. Both were confined to the Tower of London.

Cromwell claimed More had also given advice to the Holy Maid of Kent, Elizabeth Barton, who had prophesied that Henry would die if he remarried. She even claimed she had seen the place in hell that was reserved for him. She was accused of treason in January along with thirteen of her supporters, including More and Fisher. Fisher was later pardoned after being imprisoned and More proved his innocence by producing a letter which clearly showed he had in fact warned her not to meddle with state affairs. While More and Fisher were still in trouble in relation to the Act of Succession, they were cleared of involvement with Elizabeth Barton. But she had gone too far. Husee informed Lisle that on 20 April 1534 she was executed, 'hanged and headed' at Tyburn, along with two Observant Friars, two monks and one secular priest.

Henry was not a man to be thwarted and his descent into tyranny had already begun. His personal life too was a shambles. There were rumours around this time that Anne Boleyn was pregnant, as Taylor told Lisle she had 'a goodly belly',[15] and the king's visit to Calais was put off because of her pregnancy. Chapuys also mentioned the pregnancy in his dispatches in January and July, but by September he was writing: 'Since the King began to doubt whether his lady was enceinte or not, he has renewed and increased the love he formerly had for a beautiful damsel of the court.'[16] There is very little evidence for this pregnancy, which may have been a phantom one as Chapuys concluded, but more likely ended in a miscarriage. And the king was beginning to take his pleasures elsewhere.

Several courtiers were ill in April, possibly with the sweating sickness, including Lord Sandys, Captain of Guisnes, and there was a suggestion that Lisle might be able to change his role at Calais for this easier one in the Pale. Sandys rarely came to France and deputised his role from England. That Lisle would consider such a move shows that Calais was already wearing on him after only a year in the role. He wanted to go home but Lord Sandys rallied and the hope – albeit at the expense of his death – was dashed.

Lisle continued his work of rebuilding the fortifications at Calais and removing the sand hills on the east side of the town so there was no place for an invading army to hide. He heard from Sir William Fitzwilliam that Henry was pleased with this initiative and sent on his 'right hearty thanks'.[17] Fitzwilliam also broached the king on the subject of the retinue wages that Cromwell had promised to put in order but were still not paid in May. The Council wrote to the king in July to detail more work that needed doing to defend Calais and the Pale from the sea, and to make their claim that the costs had to be borne by the Crown as 'the whole country doth refuse to bear any charge for defence of the sea', but they had a plan to keep expenditure down. It appears that the area being fortified had tenants from which the king would lose rent if they were displaced, but they would not put up a fight in having to leave. The French had burnt their houses before and they had rebuilt them but did 'always fear the danger that may fall'.[18]

Lisle had heard from several people that the king was planning to visit Calais this year and everything needed to be put in order. Bryan told him it would most likely be in August, and in June Rokewood wrote to tell him that the town should be well victualled against his coming and to make sure the town was clean and free of disease. Henry was notoriously panicky about ill health, especially the sweating sickness that often swept through England. If anyone in the town had a contagious or dangerous sickness, they were to be removed. When Ryngeley had an audience with the king the first thing Henry asked was whether Calais was 'clean without sickness'.[19]

While Lisle prepared the town, his thoughts turned to his own lands. He nearly fell out with his old friend Sir William Kingston when he decided to have trees cut down at his estate in Painswick to raise much needed funds by the sale of wood and timber. Kingston, who lived at Painswick, wanted the trees to continue growing and offered him 'ready money for it',[20] as he 'loved it so well to destroy it'.[21] Lisle must have written a defensive letter to him because Kingston replied it was 'a strange letter and to me nothing pleasant'.[22] Perhaps Lisle had heard other rumours and considered his friend to be meddling in his affairs, but he was quick to reply to his 'so long familiar acquaintance' that he should 'neither have eaten nor yet slept quietly' until the situation was remedied. And as Lisle told him, 'it was forgotten on my behalf, praying you it may be so on yours: And that we may hear the one from the other after our old accustomed wont. And ye shall have me after the old fashion.'[23] Kingston was allowed a warrant for 400 trees.

A not so easy to remedy relationship was that with Sir Richard Whethill, the mayor of Calais, which would now blow out of all proportion. In 1531

Henry had granted his son Robert the next vacancy in the retinue. The grant stated that Henry VIII:

> Do give and grant unto our trusty and well-beloved Robert Whethill the room of a spear or man of war on horseback of that our retinue within our town of Calais which in any manner wise shall first or next fall void, by death, demission, resignation, forfeiture or otherwise.[24]

The position came with the 'fees, wages and rewards' granted to spears and commanded the Lord Deputy 'to accept, take and admit the said Robert Whethill'[25] when a room became available, but by 1533 his father was complaining that he still hadn't been given it. It came to a head in 1534 when Whethill followed Lisle into his garden and raged at him. The matter had become personal. Cromwell's advice was to put both father and son in prison, something in reality Lisle could not do. This was the mayor who was well respected in Calais and the argument caused a divide between those who lived and worked in the garrison town.

Lady Whethill took it upon herself to go to court in May this year and complain to the king about Lisle. Bryan had received correspondence from his friend and, hearing he was being slandered, wrote off to him quickly in September from Woodstock where he was with the king.

> I perceive that there is a certain variance betwixt young Whethill and your lordship concerning the Spear's room that John Cheyney had, which as I understand you have given unto one Wynebank who, as your lordship saith, hath done the king good service. The said Whethill pretendeth to have abill signed for a Spear's room of the next avoidance. And whereas your lordship saith that the said Whethill saith that he hath a bill signed only for Highfield's room or any privy seal, whereby it appeareth that he hath it for Highfield's room or any other. I have moved the King's Highness to know his pleasure herein… and his Grace willed me to write unto you that his pleasure is ye shall suffer the said Wynebank to continue in the said room until such time as you shall know further of his grace's pleasure on your behalf.[26]

Robert Whethill had been at court too and was also slandering Lisle. Bryan cautioned his friend:

The said Whethill saith the contents of your letters be not true, and he will prove the same by sufficient record and witness. Wherefore mine advice and counsel is, ye send hother as shortly as you can some honest man further to open and declare unto the King's Highness your demeanour towards the said Whethill, with a bill signed with the hands of them which heard the words betwixt your lordship and him.[27]

Lisle's man Husee also kept him up-to-date with news from court and warned him that the Whethills had friends in high places but that Bryan and Norris, 'your lordship's unfeigned friends',[28] were doing their best to help him. They had also counselled that he obey the king's letters as Lisle would do, but the complaints against him rumbled on.

Letters he received from Husee and Bryan at this point all contain warnings. Lisle had written to Norris about the situation and sworn that if Whethill got his room then he would give up his post and return to England, but Norris had shown Cromwell the letter bringing Husee to warn him 'a man need take heed what he write'.[29] He also reminded his master to keep what he wrote to him a secret. Bryan told his friend to 'be merry', but he also offered the advice that Lisle should 'shew yourself to be the King's officer and be not afraid of no man in doing right and justice, telling Lisle that 'amity bindeth' him to write so plainly he also advised him to look to his household as 'you are no good husband in keeping of your house, which is a great undoing of many men'.[30] Bryan is referring to Honor and the rumours that suggested she was the force behind Lisle's decisions and that it was her fault when men were dismissed. She was thought to be far more involved in the affairs of Calais than she ought to be. More worryingly, she was also thought of as being superstitious – heeding to the old religious ways.

Honor knew there was talk and wanted to know who was spreading rumours about her. William Popley, working as clerk for Cromwell, tried to allay her fears telling her he knew of no report and assuring her that Cromwell, although he tended to write plainly, 'meaneth no ill will towards your ladyship',[31] yet others – whoever they were – were suggesting she meddled too much in men's affairs. Later in the year Honor would receive a letter from Cromwell himself that stated:

I am informed that report hath been made unto you that I should be displeased with your ladyship, where of truth I know no cause wherefore I should so be. Wherefore I pray you give no such credence ne belief to any person, for your good ladyship using yourself in all causes none otherwise than I hear that ye do, and as I dobt not that ye will hereafter continue, shall find me ready to do you any pleasure that may lie in me to do as any friend that ye have[32]

But for all Cromwell's words, he also thought Honor played too much of a role in the affairs of Calais.

Husee had caught up with Cromwell to discuss several of Lisle's issues and while talking, one Henry Tourney, a member of the retinue, walked by. Cromwell remarked: 'Yonder cometh a man whom my lord has put out of wages, wherein he hath not done well.'[33] Lisle had in fact sent him to Cranmer for something not clearly stated but appears to relate to the reading of heretical books and when Husee explained, Cromwell retorted he should advise his master not to meddle in such matters. It was expected that Tourney would return and Lisle should give him back his room. In a later letter Husee reminded his master to make sure a room was vacant for him, otherwise 'you shall conceive high displeasure and lose some of your best friends'.[34] He did return to Calais but Lisle's issue with Tourney would raise its head again. The problems that occurred during this year would result in a commission hearing the following year where Lisle would be accused of selling rooms and taking bribes.

When Cromwell contacted Lisle next it was to put an end to the issue over Wingfield's Marsh. The Council was given permission to take down existing houses and make sure the area was defensible for the 'wealth, strength and commodity'[35] of Calais. The pulling down of houses did not go without problems and there were complaints, including that in one house containing a sick woman the men tasked with the job said 'they would cast down the house upon her bed, also did cast dirt and mire in the face of her chyldyr so spitefully'.[36] Wingfield, who was in England, was suitably unimpressed but wrote to Lisle that he made no complaint because he trusted he would see recompense for the destruction of his properties. No mention is made of his tenants who were forced to find new dwellings, but he himself wanted all to know 'how cruelly I am and have been dealt with'.[37] By the end of December the area was back under water, but Wingfield was not going to let it rest. He wrote several letters to Cromwell over the next few months detailing how well he had served his king, how he would do anything for the king's high pleasure and grace and how it was his duty to obey, but he also reiterated how badly he had been treated. He never outwardly blamed Lisle for the loss of his land and destruction of his property but Wingfield obviously resented him for what had happened, and the 'hindrance and extreme loss, and also exceeding shame'[38] he had endured.

Another loss that John Cheriton informed Lisle of was the *Mary Plantagenet* ship. He had heard she had sunk off the coast off France and his letter is his usual lament of being 'undone for ever and liken to die for thought',[39] but in this case he was wrong and the ship finally returned to Southampton that autumn. Now under new management and named the *Mary of Hampton*, Lisle had no more concerns with the ship. Cheriton, however, will make another appearance further on in Lisle's story.

After the trouble with Tourney earlier in the year, it seems that disgruntled members of the retinue had learned that they could go over Lisle's head if they were dismissed, by going directly to Cromwell and bringing their cause for complaint to England instead of it being treated by the Council of Calais. Although the rooms were well sort after, wages were always late, supplies were always low and the retinue, as in past times, had its disgruntled members.

Richard Hunt had taken the case of his dismissal before Cromwell and in due course Lisle received a letter from him that marvelled why. It's strange that Cromwell would constantly question Lisle over these decisions. It was part of his remit as deputy and it was obvious that Lisle had done nothing underhand or without reasonable cause, and so he made it clear in his response to the secretary. Richard Hunt's service was 'notorious', as Lisle explained:

A few years past he caused two men to come out of England hither and here to forswear themselves in his behalf, willingly, as it is here well known to all the inhabitants of this town. And they both, like perjured persons, wore papers and stood openly upon the scaffold and were then banished this town and marches.[40]

The man made a false oath to the Marshal and he was required to bring in his proof, but without licence from Lisle he had left Calais. It isn't clear exactly what he had done that he and his companions were lying about, although in another letter Lisle mentions robbery. He obviously felt strongly about the situation as in a postscript added to the letter he adds:

> Sir, what surmise or information soever he hath made you, his demeanings and doings are right well here known for naught, and detestable both to God and man.[41]

Hunt was sent back to Calais at Cromwell's behest, though it appears he was not reinstated and so returned to England where later Husee would report he was going to lodge a complaint against the deputy; it seems the matter ended there. Lisle had yet again proved that he had acted in accordance with his role, despite Cromwell's suggestion to the contrary.

As Lord Deputy he also had to entertain visiting dignitaries and in November the French Great Admiral de Brion arrived in Calais on his way to England to cement Anglo-French relations and to discuss a possible marriage between the Duke of Angouleme, the third son of Francis I, and the Princess Mary. Henry VIII would counter with a marriage to Princess Elizabeth, but in the end neither would be agreed.

Both Lisle and Honor pulled out all the stops to make sure the admiral and his entourage were well fed and entertained, and were rewarded by the assurance that 'there was never man made such good report to the King' as de Brion had done in their honour. In gratitude Honor was to receive a gift of:

> Two marmosets, the smaller ones; and the larger is a long-tailed monky which is a pretty beast and gentle ... the said beasts eat only apples and little nuts, or almonds, and you should instruct those who have charge of them that they give them only milk to drink, but it should be a little warmed. The larger beast should be kept near the fire, and the two smaller ones should always be hung up for the night close to the chimney in their boite de nuit, but during the day one may keep them caged out of doors.[42]

Honor's love of animals was well known and she often received gifts such as a parrot from Monsieur de Harchie to add to her menagerie but Lisle, who also entertained the admiral on his return visit, had more practical matters on his mind and instructed Husee to ask his friend Sir Francis Bryan if he could get him something in the way of compensation for this costly visit. He had provided lodgings for de Brion and 'made a good full supper for all the noblemen'[43] on several occasions, as well as lending them horses and mules. Bryan said he would not meddle. Basically it was something lord deputies had to do and had to pay for. But Lisle was sliding far into debt and although the visit had been a huge success in maintaining cordial French relations, his mounting financial instability was just one more reason why he wanted to return home.

Chapter Five

The Trouble with Calais
1535

L isle heard from his friend Sir William Fitzwilliam that spring. Their mutual acquaintance Rokewood was looking for the position of searcher of Oye Sluice in the Pale and Fitzwilliam had approached the king on his behalf, but the king knew that Rokewood already held the position of bailly or bailiff. Henry exclaimed: 'Well, think you that it is meet that I shall put both the baillyship and the searchership in one man's hands? No, I will not!' It didn't matter how much you were in favour with the king – he did not give out positions and grants easily. Henry was still planning on visiting Calais and Lisle looked forward to approaching him about this and other matters in person.

Another example of the issues over retinue rooms raised its head when John Worth wrote to tell Lisle that he was in England and sick. He complained that it was rumoured he left Calais without licence, that he was in debt and would sell his room. He feared Lisle would take his position from him but he swore he would 'never sell it nor give it to no man during the time your Lordship is there the King's Deputy of Calais'.[1] It appears that Lisle had gone out of his way to make sure Worth had a room and it may have been at the expense of another soldier, William Coton, who had also been allowed a room by the king sixteen years ago. He had originally been an archer and was seeking promotion to the position of spear as per the king's benefice, failing that he wanted his old room as archer back and this was granted. Worth had also been in a position where he was paid 6d a day like Coton and he tried to get Cromwell to get him a promotion by promising him a great horse and gifts of Picardy cheeses 'to desire my lord lyell to change my vj^d by the day into viij^d by the day, when any such chance shall happen to be void',[2] but perhaps because of his attempt to force Lisle's hand, he never did get promoted.

These were all daily issues he had to deal with but Lisle was aware that the political situation in Europe was unstable and he kept Cromwell informed of any rumours such as Charles V's movements with an army of 3,000 men. There was still a concern that the Holy Roman Emperor and Queen Katherine's nephew, would attack England in support of his aunt. Instead, Charles was mustering his men to launch a campaign against the Turks that would culminate in the conquest of Tunis later in the year.

Following on from the 1534 Act of Supremacy, the reformation of religion in England was building apace. Lisle was uncertain about the changes taking place and he had heard that Hugh Latimer, Bishop of Worcester, had preached an unconventional sermon before the king. Latimer was a controversial figure who had previously received a warning from Wolsey for his reformist views and his preaching that the bible should be translated in to English. Lisle had heard that:

He preached before the King's Highness, 'knowledging the Pope's authority to be the highest authority on earth, and if he shall misuse himself he ought to be reformed by a General Council and none otherwise. He also confessed our lady and holy saints most necessary to be honoured and prayed unto and that pilgrimage is very acceptable unto Almighty God...[3]

Lisle asked Cromwell to confirm if he had really preached such a sermon and if so whether the messenger who was spreading this news should be punished or not. There is no extant response from Cromwell but it is hardly likely that Latimer, a man known for his reformist leanings and a firm supporter of the king's marriage to Anne Boleyn, would have said such things. That he remained Bishop of Worcester till 1539 shows that he still held the king's trust and it was only then that his opposition of the Six Articles would see him imprisoned. It would be much later in Mary I's reign that he would suffer the ultimate punishment for his beliefs – beliefs that were contrary to Mary's devout Catholicism.

Lisle would write again to check on religious matters when a number of nuns living in the Pale decided to leave and return to their countries of birth because they would not 'be obedient to the King's Act'.[4] He could not let them leave until an inventory had been taken of their goods and he heard from Cromwell the best course of action. Even this early in his career as Lord Deputy, Lisle was wary of making decisions, especially on the matter of religion, without Cromwell's advice. Something that would be of vital importance in the coming years.

For now, Lisle and Honor knew that their home was still to be in Calais in the near future, regardless of whether Lisle was hankering to return to England. Lisle's friendships with French officers continued and when the lieutenant of Boulogne, Jacques de Coucy, lost his falcon which had flown towards Calais, he wrote to Lisle to look out for him. He would know him, he said, by the three tail feathers he had missing and the 'imping', or repair, of its broken tail, plus he wore no varvels, which are the identifying rings found on such birds. The falcon must have been precious to him because he asked Lisle if he had no knowledge of his bird to ask around and make others aware he was missing.

In March Husee began to look for permission for the Lisles to move into the Staple Inn – one of Calais' most prominent buildings. The merchants of the Staple had returned 'their place called the Staple Inn, at Calais, with the chapel, garden, and edifices on the same newly by them built, reserving only their hall in the market place, where they keep their courts and their prison house',[5] in lieu of the £16,000 worth of debt they had accrued.

The Staple Inn was one of the most impressive buildings in the town, so much so that the king himself stayed there on his way to the Field of the Cloth of Gold and it had provided lodging for the French king, Francis I, in 1532, when Henry took Anne Boleyn to meet him. It was a substantial building with myriad rooms for a large household including a Great Chamber, a Great Parlour, dining chambers, bed chambers, a chapel, an armoury, counting house, bakehouse and brewhouse and would make excellent accommodation for Lisle and his growing household.

For the time being nothing would happen to further Lisle's causes as Cromwell was sick, or feigning it as the Spanish ambassador, Chapuys, believed. While Husee waited to talk to the secretary, he heard from Lisle that it was rumoured Husee would not return to Calais, 'that I should leave the key under the door and come no more there', as he had not paid his rent. He assured his master that he knew that the only reason he was in England was concerning 'your causes and affairs, some of which are weighty', and if Lisle wanted him back in Calais, he would return, for there was 'one thing your lordship may be well assured of, and that is me, with the uttermost I can do'.[6] This year he would be granted a place in 'le constablerie' of the Calais garrison with a daily wage of 8d. Husee would always remain faithful and true to his master and he obviously made every effort to resolve Lisle's issues as come April he had managed to see Cromwell and sent Lisle the news that the Staple Inn had been agreed as his new home.

Lisle sorely needed his revenue and 'creation money', but it was not yet forthcoming. Leonard Smyth had been Lisle's man up to this point but entered Cromwell's service in January. He informed him that it was not 'barred or taken' from him and that it was proving difficult to raise funds from the sheriffs of the shires for 'fines, issues and americaments (penalties)'. He was not the only one not receiving his dues and as Smyth put it, 'you are in no worse case therefore than all the other noblemen'[7] who also received such payments.

Lisle at this time wrote several letters concerning Sir Edward Ryngeley and his complaints against him. He had not been able to build a relationship with this prominent member of the Council and Ryngeley had sold his position as High Marshal of Calais for £400 to Sir Richard Grenville, Lisle's nephew through his marriage to Honor. Grenville had actively sought the position, but why the prospect of such a role appealed to him is a mystery as Ryngeley certainly had nothing good to say about it. Grenville must have known of Lisle's difficulties, although at this point they were nothing compared to what they would become.

With Ryngeley in England, Lisle feared that his words would be taken as his incompetence at managing the affairs of Calais. Ryngeley, he said, was angry with him for easing the watches and allowing the town to decay. They had particularly fallen out over a man, Fryer, who Ryngeley had made keeper of the prison on the walls but whom Lisle knew to be a thief and so refused to allow him on the watch and give him the 'watchword'. Writing to Cromwell and his friend Fitzwilliam, he iterated that it would be best if he explained to the king in person. But the king did not give Lisle a licence to return to England and there was no sign of him coming to Calais.

Someone who did return to Calais was Ryngeley who wished to conclude his affairs, and Lisle, although dreading him pursuing any further complaints against him, treated the man with respect and dignity.

He thanked him for his service and offered him lodgings should he and his wife ever wish to visit Calais again, although Ryngeley didn't miss the town where he had spent so much time and thought he would never return. He added: 'If I have been blunt to you at any time I am sure it hath been for your honour, for I never meant worse to you than to myself…',[8] and for now their relationship was amicable.

A relationship that was souring, however, was that between Leonard Smyth and the Lisles. He still continued to manage some of Lisle's affairs in England and it was hoped that with him being closer to the king's secretary Smyth would promote his master's causes, but this would be the last year of any of his correspondence to Lisle and it does not appear that the hope vested in him was ever warranted. A letter he would send to Honor later this year stated that he 'perceived suspicion in your ladyship towards me long since, which moved me the less to meddle in any of your causes'.[9] As with several of their relationships that became written correspondence rather than personal meetings, wires got crossed and rumours were spread by other people. Smyth said:

I defy all those that can report of me unto my lord or your ladyship or lay unto my charge one point or spot of falsehood, concealment or deceit by me towards my lord or you ever done or thought. But I have beaten divers bushes and other have taken the birds.[10]

On a more humorous note, Honor had sent Lord Edmund Howard a remedy for a kidney stone. Howard was the father of Henry's fifth queen, Catherine Howard, and at this time comptroller of Calais. His letter telling her he had taken her remedy to drastic effect follows in full, not only to show a side of Honor that acted as physician but also for its delightful content!

Madame, so it is I have this night after midnight taken your medicine, for the which I heartily thank you, for it hath done me much good, and hath caused the stone to break, so that now I void much gravel. But for all that, your said medicine hath done me little honesty, for it made me piss my bed this night, for the which my wife hath sore beaten me, and saying it is children's parts to be piss their bed. Ye have made me such a pisser that I dare not this day go

abroad, wherefore I beseech you to make mine excuse to my Lord
and Master Treasurer, for that I shall not be with you this day at
dinner. Madame, it is showed me that a wing or a leg of a stork,
if I eat thereof, will make me that I shall never piss more in bed,
and though my body be simple yet my tongue shall ever be good,
and especially when it speaketh of women; and sithence such a great
medicine will do a great cure God send me apiece thereof.[11]

While Honor was trying to help her fellow Calisiens, Lisle had been busy
overseeing new ordnance for the defence of Calais, so at some point funds
must have been forthcoming after his report in 1533. Thirty-two pieces
were finished with twelve more in production. Lisle had heard them shot
on May Day and wrote to the king in excitement that he had 'never heard
vehementer pieces'. He was full of praise for Henry Johnson who had
undertaken the work, including installing each tower with arquebuses and
'other pieces convenient, saving the vaults'.[12] The Beauchamp and Dublin
Towers had been repaired with new platforms and Newnhambridge and
Hammes had been stocked with shot.

He was soon caught up again with another problem of rooms as
well. Henry Tourney, who been allowed back into the retinue after the
difficulties he caused the previous year, was now in trouble again. It is
not clearly stated what he had done, but again it appears to be something
of a religious nature and he was also disgruntled about his loss of wages
and this time he was banished from Calais. His room became vacant and
a kinsman of Sir Henry Knyvet, Edward Clifford, had been granted his
place by the king. Although Henry admitted that was as long as he hadn't
already given it to someone else!

Clifford wasn't sure whether to carry on to Calais or await further
instructions when he met Tourney at the English sea port of Dover;
Tourney appeared to be waiting to cross the Channel, even though
he had not only been dismissed from the retinue but the town as well.
Tourney was not giving up his place without a fight and was airing his
unhappiness to all who would listen.

Lisle, for his part, was becoming increasingly frustrated with the king
and Cromwell and their involvement in matters that were assigned to
him as Lord Deputy. He told Cromwell: 'I should never be able to serve
the King in executing any ordinance, but that every man hereby would

be encouraged to speak at large, so that I were better be out of the world than bear office, if the ordinances be once broken.'[13]

In a further letter he reminds Cromwell it was he who told him to give Tourney's room to Clifford, which was done 'all only by your letter', and he concludes:

It may please the King's Highness to direct his honourable letters to the commissioners that cometh here, to hear the matter, and to know whether the said Torney hath been ordered otherwise than right and good conscience would, whereby it shall be known to his Majesty whether the same proceeded of malice or not.[14]

But the king's mind was elsewhere and in England that summer there would be events that would shock the nation. On 22 June 1535, John Fisher, who had once been Bishop of Rochester, was executed on Tower Hill. Fisher had been a firm supporter of Queen Katherine of Aragon and refused to take the Oath of Succession and accept Henry as the Supreme Head of the Church of England. He had been accused of treason and towards his end it was believed he had also been conspiring to overthrow the king through Charles V, and he included Lisle's kinswoman and her son in his plans. Chapuy's informed the Holy Roman Emperor:

That excellent and holy man, the bishop of Rochester, told me some time ago, the Pope's weapon become very malleable when directed against the obdurate and pertinacious, and, therefore, it is incumbent upon Your Majesty to interfere in this affair, and undertake a work which must be as pleasing in the eyes of God as war upon the Turk. Indeed, should there be a question of coming to a rupture [with England] it would not be amiss for Your Majesty to try by all possible means to have at your court, or elsewhere under your power, the son of the Princess' governess [Margaret], the daughter of the duke of Clarence [George], upon whom, in the opinion of many people here, the succession to the Grown would by right devolve. Owing to the said Duke's great and singular virtues, her son [Reginald Pole] is now studying at the Paduan University, to which circumstance may be added that being closely related to this king, both on the fathers and mother's side, he and his brothers might easily lay claim to the succession to the kingdom. For this reason the Queen wishes for a marriage in that quarter as much, or perhaps more than in any other, and the Princess herself; far from refusing it, would, I have no doubt, gladly give her consent. The youth and his brothers have many relatives and allies [among the nobility] besides a very numerous party whose affections Your Majesty might by such means easily gain, and thus secure those of the rest of this nation.[15]

Then on 1 July 1535, Sir Thomas More's trial began. He was found guilty under the Treason Act of 1534 which stated:

If any person or persons, after the first day of February next coming, do maliciously wish, will or desire, by words or writing, or by craft imagine, invent, practise, or attempt any bodily harm to be done or committed to the king's most royal person, the queen's, or their heirs apparent, or to deprive them or any of them of their dignity, title, or name of their royal estates.[16]

On 6 July 1535, More was sentenced to be hanged, drawn and quartered, but the King commuted it to beheading. Husee, usually so vocal on affairs in England, doesn't tell of Fisher or More's execution and neither does any other correspondent. This was a matter too dangerous to discuss.
    Hall's Chronicle related:

About Nine he was brought out of the Tower; his Beard was long, his face pale and thin, and carrying a Red Cross in his Hand, he often lift up his Eyes to Heaven; a Woman meeting him with a cup of Wine, he refused it saying, Christ at his Passion drank no wine, but Gall and Vinegar. Another Woman came crying and demanded some Papers she said she had left in his Hands, when he was Lord Chancellor, to whom he said, Good woman, have Patience but for an Hour and the King will rid me of the Care I have for those Papers, and every thing else. Another Woman followed him, crying, He had done her much Wrong when he was Lord Chancellor, to whom he said, I very well remember the Cause, and is I were to decide it now, I should make the same Decree.

When he came to the Scaffold, it seemed ready to fall, whereupon he said merrily to the Lieutenant, Pray, Sir, see me safe up; and as to my coming down, let me shift for myself. Being about to speak to the People, he was interrupted by the Sheriff, and thereupon he only desired the People to pray for him, and bear Witness he died in the Faith of the Catholic Church, a faithful Servant both to God and the King. Then kneeling, he repeated the Miserere Psalm with much Devotion; and, rising up the Executioner asked him Forgiveness. He kissed him, and said, Pick up thy Spirits, Man, and be not afraid to do thine Office; my Neck is very short, take heed therefore thou strike not awry for having thine Honesty. Laying his Head upon the Block, he bid the Executioner stay till he had put his Beard aside, for that had committed no Treason. Thus he suffered with much Cheerfulness; his Head was taken off at one Blow, and was placed upon London-Bridge, where, having continued for some Months, and being about to be thrown into the Thames to make room for others, his Daughter Margaret bought it, inclosed it in a Leaden Box, and kept it for a Relique.[17]

If Lisle had taken anything from More's death, it should have been to know that it didn't matter how close you were to the king, he could order your death in an instant. Even though Lisle was the king's uncle, as his story unfolds, we can see they were not overly close. Henry treated him like the servant he was, even though he had no other living uncles or aunts at the time. His younger sister Mary was dead and he had a tumultuous relationship with his elder sister Margaret in Scotland. If Henry felt any ties of kinship, he kept his feelings close to his chest.

Cromwell was also in a testy mood at this time and when Husee had delivered Lisle's most recent correspondence to him, he had replied in such a manner that Husee could not commit to paper what he had said but would tell Lisle when he next came to Calais. The king's secretary had heard more rumours about the garrison town and sent him a warning to 'not write any news but those which you know to be certain; and whatsoever he writ your lordship is not to be passed on so earnestly as your lordship is wont to do'.[18] We get a sense that Cromwell was weary with Lisle always asking for advice and perhaps passing on rumours before he knew they were fact. It would be better if he made sure of his aspersions before he wrote, for as Husee said, Cromwell's 'anger lasteth in such causes but a while'.[19]

When Lisle needed to escape, he stayed out of town at 'a place of mine, three mile out of Calais',[20] as he did now. The place was a farm in all its rural simplicity as a later inventory detailed. That it was a working farm is clear from the kitchen's contents which included cheese presses, churns, boiling vats, butter tubs and cloths. There were sheep, cows and pigs on the farm. Inside was a simple layout furnished with cushions, covers, carpets, stools, a feather bed and other mattresses with plain cloths, napkins and towels. A humble dwelling for the couple to retreat to and contemplate their life away from the busy town.

As soon as he was back, Lisle had to deal with an incident that had taken place in the town. One Adrian Skell had been drinking and offered a John Ansley a pot of beer, but Ansley refused to drink 'with no such Fleming or Picard'.[21] Taking offence, Skell attacked Ansley with a staff, beating him around the head until he fell dead beside his horse. Husee explained the situation to the king and told Lisle:

> If your lordship handle him well it is not to be doubted but he will pay well for it, for the King's Highness thinketh that at least it will be worth ₵ li to you.[22]

So a pardon for manslaughter could profit both Lisle and the king when the offender paid for his pardon and a third of his goods became forfeit to the king. Husee was suffering from sciatica but over the coming months he did manage to get Skell's pardon. Skell remained in prison from July to December before his release. Although it seems a corrupt system, it was legal and approved by the king.

Something that was also approved by the king, and may have worried Lisle, was the royal commission that was ordered to investigate the state of Calais and its retinue. For six weeks Sir William Kingston; Thomas Walsh, Baron of the Exchequer; John Baker, Attorney of the Duchy of Lancaster; George Paulet and Anthony St Leger would look into the issues that Calais faced, including the retinue and defences, the amount of strangers in the town, houses in decay and the behaviour of Calais' administrators – its officers, ministers and soldiers – 'to reform all matters relating to the safe custody and defence of the town and marches of

Calais, and of the castles of Guysnes, Hammes, Rysbank, Newingham Bridge, Mark, and Oye'.[23]

Although Ryngeley and Lisle had parted on amicable terms, Ryngeley had given Cromwell a report on the state of Calais and Lisle felt compelled to write a list of articles for the commissioners that addressed Ryngeley's complaints. Lisle started by saying: 'I do know that Sir Edward Ryngeley, Knight, High Marshal here, hath delivered a book touching the wealth of this town, which book I desire you that I may be called unto to make answer'.[24]

The commissioners had every intention of interviewing Lisle about his role as Lord Deputy but he wanted to particularly address points such as soldiers of the retinue having second jobs, houses being thatched when tiles or slates would be safer, and as we saw with the Skell case, strangers in the town. There was obviously some racist sentiment, but it was compounded by the way in which the Council set rules on the trading of goods and whether they allowed strangers licence to marry into English families. Lisle ended his articles with a list of those to whom he had given rooms. Ryngeley had brought up the subject of rooms too, and insinuated that Lisle took bribes and mismanaged who were granted positions in the retinue.

The commissioners did a thorough job, interviewing people and assessing the situation. They were charged to look into almost every aspect of Calais life from retinue numbers, the order of the watches, the admission and trading of strangers, fire precautions taken as in vessels of water at every man's door, victualling, the value of goods and land, clerical absenteeism and last but by no means least the issue of retinue rooms.

They reported to Cromwell that they found the town 'far out of order', and that 'it would grieve and pity the heart of any good and true Englishman to hear or see the same',[25] but they also informed him that they could not change everything there and then and that an Act of Parliament would be needed.

The changes enshrined in the Act of Calais, one of the 'mooste pryncipall treasours belonging to this the realme of England',[26] would be passed by parliament the following year. It confirmed the Lord Deputy's authority and the role of the Council, including revised oaths for the Lord Deputy and principal officers, the composition, numbers and wages of the retinue, and a ban on them having secondary employment. The selling of rooms was now forbidden.

Lisle's expanded oath really underlined the changes that had occurred in England and the changes in the king's temperament accentuated by a sense of paranoia and tyranny. It began:

> Ye shall swear that ye shall be faithful and true unto our Sovereign Lorde King Henry the Eight by the grace of God King of England and of France Defender of the faith Lorde of Ireland and in earth supreme heed of the Church of England; and if ye shall know anything that shall be prejudicial or hurtful unto his Highness or his heirs or to his Towne of Calais or Marches of the same, Ye shall resist the same to the uttermost of your power. And in case ye cannot ye shall without delay declare the same unto his Highness or to such of his Council as ye think will show it unto him.[27]

And it also underlined that he was not to be absent from his office without the king's licence – something that would come up later. As would the clause:

> Ye shall do your devoir at your power to the keeping of the peace among all estates and other persons of what degree or condition so ever they be, within the said town dwelling or thereunto from time to time repairing, not suffering any congregations, assembles, commotions or conventicles to be made within the said town against the said peace or against the good restful and politic governance of the same town. And if any persons, of what degree or condition so ever he or they be within the said Towne, that provoketh prively or apertly any such congregation, assemble commotion, sedition or conventicle as be found faulty thereof, either else that taketh upon him any unlawful maintenance to the perturbance and violation of the said peace or against right to repress by might any person, ye shall resist and let withe the advice of the residue of the King's Council of the said town and do such punishment thereunto as with reason may serve, without exception of person not sparing so to do for favour, love, dread or meed of any person.[28]

The issue of strangers or 'aliens' was addressed as was the victualling of the town and the paying of tolls and taking of customs. Religious observance was set out and it was emphasised that the English tongue should be spoken rather than French. Housing was addressed and safety precautions in case of fire as per the commission's instructions. Importantly, going forward, Calais was to be represented in Parliament by two members with the lord deputy and his council and the mayor and his council each allowed 'to nominate, elect, and choose … one able and discreet person inhabiting within the said town of Calais'.[29]

Yes, Calais had its problems, but the commission did not conclude that Lisle was to blame. The act made a blanket assertion that Calais was 'nowe of late greattely enfeebled aswell through the decayes of the edifices and buyldynges therof as also through the negligent and remysse behavours of dyvers and sondry Offycers Mynisters and Souldeours there takyng his Highnes fees'.[30]

Fitzwilliam wrote to Lisle later in the year that he had:

Made such report unto the King's said Highness of the good conformity which I have found in your lordship and other of his servants in those parts … and doubt ye not but that his Highness is and will be good and gracious lord unto you all, and intendeth to establish and do such things for the weal and surety of the town and marches as was never done not heard of before. And in the mean season the pleasure of his Highness is, that your lordship … do see that not only that the proclamations made by me and my colleagues at our late being with you be duly executed and kept, but also that the town with all diligence be victualled for half a year according to the order I and my said colleagues took in that behalf.[31]

It must have been a weight off Lisle's mind to know that not only was he cleared of any misdoings, but finally some of the issues that he had been constantly battling would appear to be over.

But come November, Lisle received a letter from the king himself. Henry wanted him to restore Tourney, who had been banished in June, to his room in the retinue. Tourney must have had friends in high places because Henry also wanted his wages restored from when he was banished and his place in the retinue to resume as normal. Lisle had not 'hitherto

Edward IV. (*Wikimedia commons, public domain*)

Medieval cap badge 'Bosworth Eagle'. (*Wikimedia Commons CC 2.0: Leicestershire City Council*)

Bust of Henry VII. (*Wikimedia Commons, CC2.5: Val_McG*)

Henry VIII by Hans Holbein. (*Wikimedia commons, public domain*)

Thomas Cromwell by Hans Holbein. (*Wikimedia commons, public domain*)

Catherine of Aragon. (*Wikimedia commons, public domain*)

Lisle's Coat of Arms. (*Wikimedia Commons, public domain*)

Portchester Castle. (*Wikimedia commons, public domain*)

A Jousting Henry VIII by Cornelis
Anthonisz (manner of), 1538–1548.
(*Rijksmuseum, public domain*)

Dover Castle. (*Wikimedia Commons, public domain*)

ANNA CLIVENSIS HENRICI VIII REGIS ANGLIÆ VXOR IIII.

Holbein pinxit   Wenceslaus Hollar fecit Aqua forti, ex Collectione Arundeliana Aᵒ 1642.

Portrait of Anne of Cleves, Wenceslaus Hollar, after Hans Holbein (II), 1649. (*Rijksmuseum, public domain*)

The Outer Walls of Calais, by Stefano della Bella, 1647. (*Rijksmuseum, public domain*)

Ships at Calais, by Stefano della Bella, 1647. (*Rijksmuseum, public domain*)

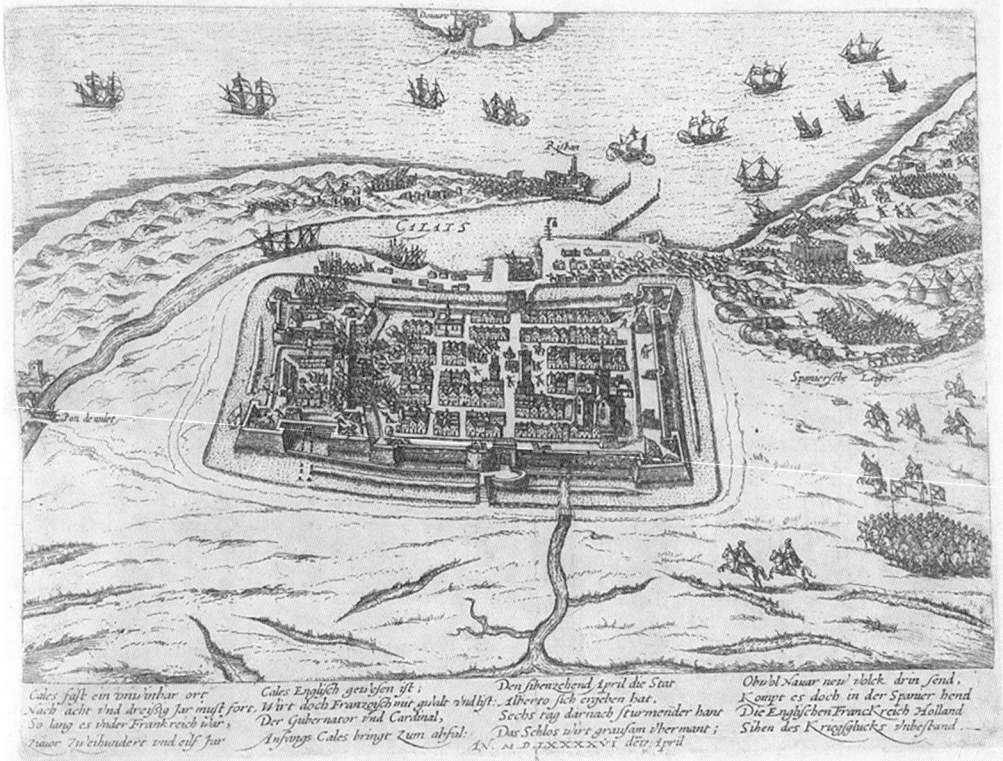

Siege of Calais 1576. (*Wikimedia commons, public domain*)

Portrait of Cardinal Reginald
Pole, by Pieter van Gunst,
after Adriaen van der Werff,
c. 1669–1731. (*Rijksmuseum,
public domain*)

A dramatic portrayal of Margaret Pole's execution. (*Wikimedia commons, public domain*)

Sir Brian Tuke. (*Wikimedia commons, public domain*)

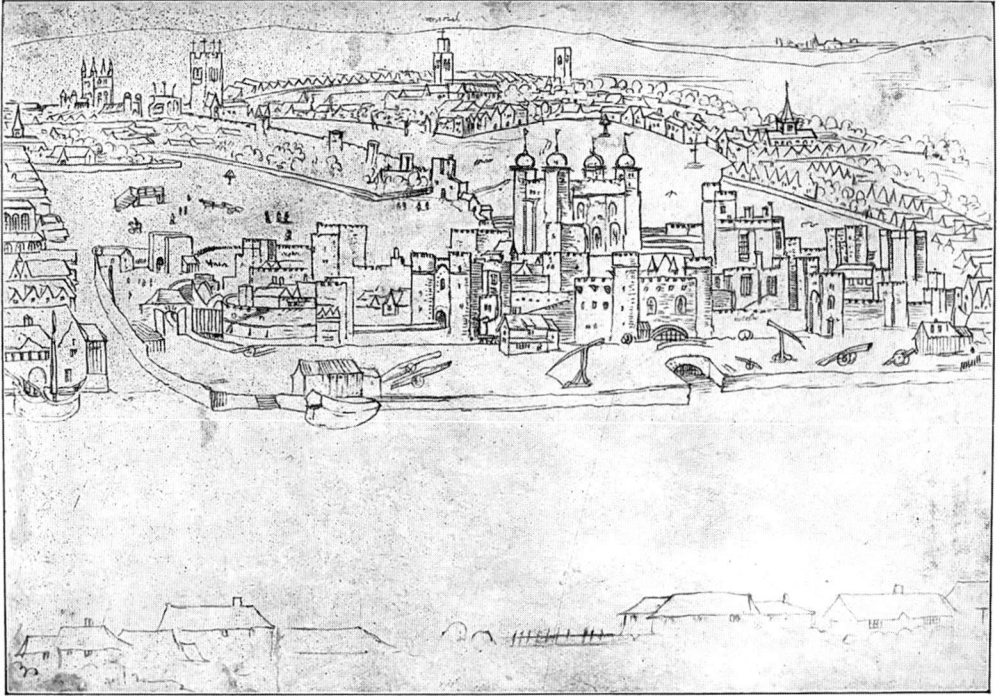

A View of the Tower of London by Antony van den Wyngaerde. (*Wikimedia Commons, public domain*)

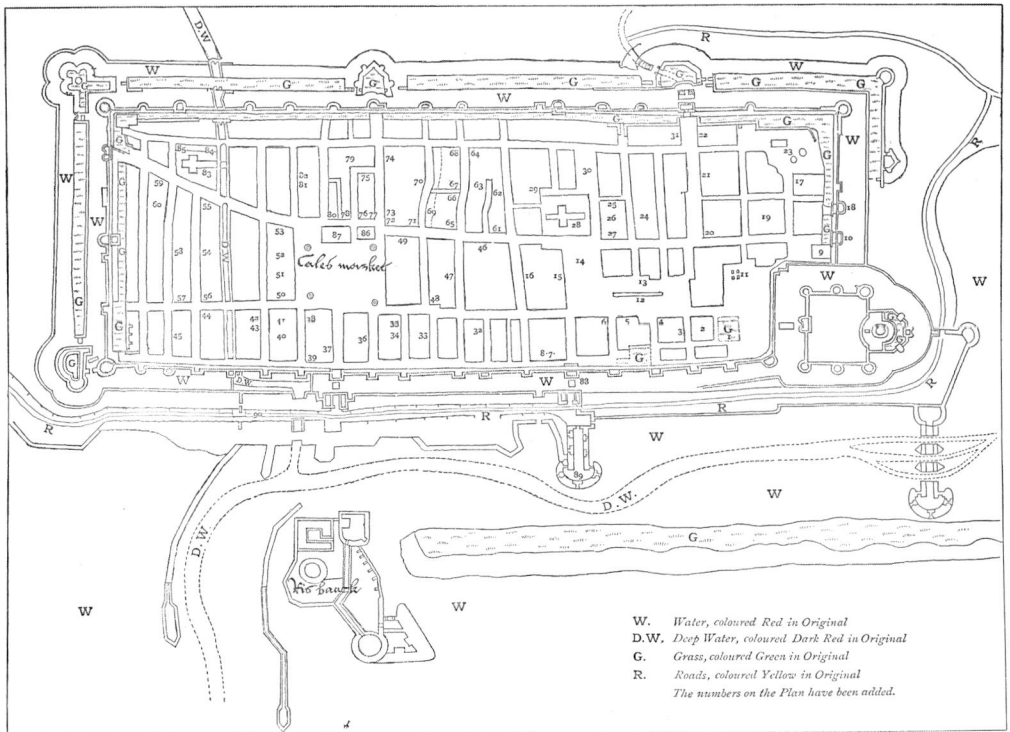

W.   Water, coloured Red in Original
D.W. Deep Water, coloured Dark Red in Original
G.   Grass, coloured Green in Original
R.   Roads, coloured Yellow in Original
      The numbers on the Plan have been added.

Fig. 4. PLAN OF CALAIS. (From *Cott. MS.* Aug. I. II. 71.)

Street Map of Calais. (*Photography courtesy of Shay Webb*)

obeyed and accomplished' this command and he was warned he would suffer the king's 'high displeasure'[32] if he did not do as he was told.

Lisle had, of course, to obey his nephew, but he didn't do it without pointing out it was 'no little grief' to his heart. Tourney, he said, never served the king and had been remiss at keeping the watch. He had not banished the man out of malice but for the good of the retinue. He pointed out to Cromwell that it was he who asked him to favour Clifford, and he who told him that it was the king's pleasure that he received Tourney's room. Lisle signs off 'written with the hand of him that had never had a heavier heart',[33] and it is a sign that Lisle was now really troubled by his role as Lord Deputy.

And the problems with the retinue did not stop there. His next letter to Cromwell details another soldier, Henry Palmer, who had caused trouble. There is a sense that now Lisle is informing Cromwell continually of the issues for fear of either complaints being made against him, or risking the king's displeasure. No matter what the commission had decided, he was still in an awkward position and the issue of the retinue and rooms would never end. Henry Palmer had wanted licence to go to England and Lisle had said no. He had committed him to the walls as punishment and underlined that what he had done was in accordance with his remit but told Cromwell, 'I beseech you not to be miscontented with my doing so, nor to give credence to any [of] his messages or writings, unto such time as I and other of the Council here shall certify you more at large the truth of everything.'[34] Lisle was covering his back – what he did, he did not do alone but in agreement with the Calais Council, but he still knew that Cromwell or the king could overturn their decision at any time. It was a no-win situation and he was becoming increasingly tired with being caught in the middle of a thankless task.

And then came Christmas; a time that perhaps Lisle was looking forward to, a time to relax and spend time with Honor and their family. He had his duties to perform, one of which on Christmas Day turned into a disaster. He was to attend church with the Council who met at his house and although they waited, Sir Robert Wingfield and Sir Richard Whethill, Mayor of Calais, did not arrive. Unable to wait any longer they continued to the church until Whethill arrived and was furious that Lisle had 'tarried not for him', to which Lisle made answer 'if there should be any tarrying he ought to tarry for me'.[35] It has all the marks of a squabble between Calais' most prominent figures, but it was more serious than that and Lisle wrote to Sir William Fitzwilliam, who had headed the commission, that it did not stop there.

> Sir, I have entertained the Mayor more than it hath become me, but Sir Robert Wingfield his malice for the drown of the marsh will not be forgotten. He said to me this Christmas that he would have me and the Porter in action for the drowning of. I made him answer, he that commanded me should save me harmless. I said I marvelled he would sit with the mayor and leave me and the King's Council chamber. He made answer he was sworn to the Mayor and burgesses, and that he would keep. And then I said, 'For your first oath, I am sure you have a dispensation'; and so I departed.[36]

These men made Lisle's life more difficult. They did not respect him and blamed him for situations out of his control. He was caught not only in the middle but on all sides and his nephew, the king, was doing nothing to help him.

Chapter Six

The Year of Three Queens
1536

Katherine of Aragon died on January 1536 at Kimbolton Castle in Cambridgeshire. Henry had sent her there to be forgotten. The damp, marshy environment had done nothing for her health. She had few servants to care for her and was never allowed to see her daughter. It was a bitter, sad and lonely end for a true and loyal queen and her lingering demise is probably one of the cruellest acts Henry VIII ever committed.

Chapuys, the Spanish ambassador, had supported Katherine as much as he could. He had seen her recently but thought her health was improving and returned to London not knowing it was the last time he would see her. He reported to her nephew Charles V, Holy Roman Emperor:

The Queen died two hours after midday, and eight hours afterwards she was opened by command of those who had charge of it on the part of the King, and no one was allowed to be present, not even her confessor or physician, but only the candle-maker of the house and one servant and a 'compagnon', who opened her, and although it was not their business, and they were no surgeons, yet they have often done such a duty, at least the principal, who on coming out told the Bishop of Llandaff, her confessor, but in great secrecy as a thing which would cost his life, that he had found the body and all the internal organs as sound as possible except the heart, which was quite black and hideous, and even after he had washed it three times it did not change colour. He divided it through the middle and found the interior of the same colour, which also would not change on being washed, and also some black round thing which clung closely to the outside of the heart. On my man asking the physician if she had died of poison he replied that the thing was too evident by what had been said to the Bishop her confessor, and if that had not been disclosed the thing was sufficiently clear from the report and circumstances of the illness.[1]

Chapuys suspected poison had hastened Katherine's death and privately he blamed the Boleyns and their supporters. When she was buried at Peterborough Abbey as a Dowager Princess, not as Queen of England, Chapuys refused to attend, disgusted at her treatment in life and now in death. Chapuys wasn't the only one that mourned the queen but no one could be seen to have any sympathy, however much they felt for her. No one wrote to Lisle of the queen's demise. Some things were too dangerous to say and definitely too dangerous to write.

Letters in Tudor England were carried by messengers and in the case of correspondence going from Calais to England and vice versa, this of course required a journey. The letter sender had to trust the messenger would deliver his correspondence safely, and pay for the costs of the messenger. Sir Brian Tuke, Treasurer of the King's Chamber, would also become the first Master of the King's Post and it was from him that Lisle received his first communication of the new year concerning the paying of messengers. Lisle had contacted the treasurer about paying these messengers before now and they had been duly paid because Lisle said he would make sure Tuke received an allowance going forward but this had never materialised. Now asking again Tuke refused, saying:

> It is strange to me to receive commandments from Calais to pay the King's money. And upon what grounds your lordship should require it of me I know not. If ye require it of me as of the Treasurer of the King's Chamber, I have no warrant to pay it. If ye require it as of him that hath oversight of the King's posts, it is nothing depending upon that charge.[2]

Lisle was falling further into debt and countered that he only did as other deputies had done, but Tuke was having none of it and told him that was simply not true. He did not have a warrant from the king to pay such messengers and Lisle would have to cover them himself. Tuke had some experience in the affairs of Calais as he had served from 1510 to 1520 as clerk of the Council there. He was no fool and could not be persuaded otherwise.

A friendlier missive arrived this year from Honor's daughter Mary to her sister Philippa. The letter accompanied gifts for them all, including a parrot for Lisle 'because he maketh much of a bird'. She asked that he send her 'some pretty thing' in return – which would probably have been delegated to Husee – but she plaintively declared that Lisle had not yet sent her anything 'although I have never forgot him'.[3] Lisle did not seem to take an active interest in his stepdaughters – or even his own for that matter, perhaps leaving their affairs to Honor to sort out. His youngest, Bridget, was largely ignored, but it was to Honor that letters arrived asking for new clothes. The abbess at Winchester had to inform her that she lacked a gown and kirtle, a partlet for her neck and coif for her head and tellingly, it is the abbess who has to tell the Lisles how long Bridget has been with her.

Following the altercation Lisle had had on Christmas day the previous year, Sir Robert Wingfield was called in front of the Council and asked if he took Lisle to be the King's Deputy and supreme head of Calais or not. Lisle informed Cromwell he gave a good answer and it seemed to be an end of the matter although Wingfield did send his version of events onto the secretary himself.

By March Lisle was reporting again to Cromwell, but on a more serious international matter. Hostilities between Charles V and Francis I were marching apace and there was every fear there would be a confrontation. Lisle reported that so far war had been proclaimed by sea but not by land.

Given the political background, Calais and the Pale needed to be defensible should conflict break out. Lisle had ridden out to Guisnes with Sir Thomas Palmer and others to check the fortifications there. There was a break in the wall and it looked like it was crumbling more every day. There was no other remedy Lisle thought, than to build another wall and he furnished Cromwell with instructions and costs for the repair.

Lisle must have been thoroughly sick of the business of the retinue and rooms but once again he was contacted by someone seeking preference. Despite heading the previous year's commission and seeking to guide the act through parliament which included a ban on the selling of rooms, Sir William Fitzwilliam wrote to Lisle seeking preference for one Richard Holmes, to whom he hoped Lisle would give first choice if a room came up. The deputy's list of men to fill such rare vacancies must have been exhaustive.

Thomas Prowde, the oldest Calais spear, died around March and Lisle granted his room to Leonard Snowden; once again he angered Sir Richard Whethill, who had asked for the room to be given to his son Robert. The same Robert who, back in 1534, was still waiting to be admitted to the retinue. Given the ongoing rows over retinue rooms, it isn't clear why Robert had still not been given a place. Perhaps Snowden was next in line and Lisle was going by the book, but Whethill was not going to let it lie and would bring the matter to Parliament, 'to have the patent allowed there by act'.[4] Lisle swore in a letter to Ralph Sadler that 'he and his son hath misued themselves towards me, working the most mischief against me they could devise; and the said Sir Richard is my enemy and always hath been since my hither coming'.[5] Even Honor had fallen foul of Lady Whethill, who had slandered her husband 'in Pilate's voice'[6] one day when she attended church.

Whethill's persistence paid off however, and he received confirmation from the king that his son should have Prowde's room. But the king had also agreed three years ago that when Prowde's room became vacant, either Sir Thomas Palmer, Ralph Broke or Thomas Tate should receive it. It had fallen to Sir Thomas Palmer who, now being Knight Porter, had the right to give it to 'any able man' – and this had been Leonard Snowden. Lisle had then acted in accordance with the king's previous wishes and here was the problem. Henry either didn't remember, or was lax in keeping any check on the rooms he granted and to whom he granted them. Perhaps that although this was a huge issue for Lisle, it was nothing to the king. Lisle was thoroughly vexed and it was made worse by the arrival of Robert Whethill, who had his permission from the king but had still not approached Lisle with it. He wrote to his nephew:

The young man whom your Grace doth write for did declare unto me openly before a hundred of your servants here, in your Gate, that he would have a Spear's room here and ask me no leave, and would give me no thanks for the same, which methinks became him evil to say, seeing that I did him no wrong. And within few days after, his father came home to my house, and began to fall out with me maintaining the saying of his son neither wisely nor discreetly but slanderously, and tempted me more than I ever was; and if I had not been your Deputy here he should well a'known his folly![7]

Lisle suggested that future appointments should be sent to the king for approval, before the deputy swore them into the retinue. But for now the ill-feeling between himself and the Whethills would continue – for Lisle they not only caused him trouble, they undermined his authority in Calais. He knew they were his enemies and felt he had done nothing to deserve such animosity.

Another relationship at risk of fracturing was that with Jehan de Tovar, Captain of Gravelines, who had imprisoned a man called Derrick and confiscated his writings. Lisle called on him to release the man so as to not irritate the king or cause any trouble between Henry VIII and Charles V. He sent a copy to Cromwell, but in his original correspondence to Tovar he added a curious postscript that alludes to the similarity they had in their births:

> Monsieur le captaine, where you set forward your birth and nobility by these your letters, few great personages are aware thereof, whereas I know well that all nobles princes and honourable gentlemen are surely informed of my extraction. And I verily believe, as do men of all estates, that if you were indeed the issue of a noble lineage, that your conditions and manners would be more honest than they are. This between you and me, to conclude my letter.[8]

It is no wonder that after all this Lisle wanted to see his nephew and explain about the Whethill affair, his debts and other matters in person. In April, he asked Cromwell for a licence to see the king when he was next at Dover. Henry agreed but didn't feel the need to put it in writing. Henry Norris, one of Lisle's supporters at court, was his witness, but just days later he was arrested and the king's visit to Dover was postponed.

The king had lately become infatuated with Jane Seymour, the daughter of Sir John Seymour and Margery Wentworth. Chapuys, the Spanish ambassador, described her as being 'of middle stature and no great beauty, so fair that one would call her rather pale than otherwise'.[9] Henry was tired of Anne Boleyn and frustrated by still having no legitimate male heir. It was said Anne had found Jane cosying up to the king and screamed at Henry: 'I saw this harlot Jane sitting on your lap while my belly was doing its duty!' Her jealousy drove her into a rage and she lost the child she was carrying.

In April 1536 Sir Francis Bryan told Jane's family: 'they should soon see his niece well-bestowed in marriage'.[10] Henry may have been interested in Jane, but up until accusations of adultery, treason and incest were brought against his queen he probably only wanted her as his mistress rather than his next wife.

On 2 May 1536, Henry Norris was taken to the Tower of London. Mark Smeaton, Sir Francis Weston, Sir William Brereton and Lord Rochford were also arrested. Sir Francis Bryan was 'sent for in all haste on his allegiance' and questioned about his relationship with Anne and what he knew of her relationships with other men, as were Thomas Wyatt and Richard Page, who both spent some time in the Tower but were never charged.

On the same day, a messenger was sent to Anne Boleyn telling her her presence was required by the Privy Council. There she was informed that she was being accused of committing adultery with three different men and that Smeaton and Norris had already confessed.

Lisle had heard the news of his friend's arrest by 8 May, as he adds in a letter to Cromwell:

> and seeing there are many things now in his gracious disposition and hands, by reason of the most mischievous, heinous, and most abominable treasons against his most gracious and royal crown and person committed, I wholly trusts that his Grace, being good lord unto me, will vouchsafe to employ some part of those same upon me.[11]

Which is basically Lisle putting himself forward for some of the spoils. It may seem unsympathetic, but it was a typical way of receiving grants from the king after a person's goods and land were forfeited to the crown.

Anne had little time to ready herself before she too was taken to the Tower of London. Lisle's old friend, Sir William Kingston, Constable of the Tower of London, was charged with her care. From here, she wrote what is presumed to be her last letter to Henry, probably never even read by the king, supposedly found in Thomas Cromwell's personal belongings after his death:

> Your Grace's displeasure and my imprisonment are things so strange unto me as what to write or what to excuse I am altogether ignorant.

Whereas you sent unto me, willing me to confess a truth and so to obtain your favour, by such an one whom you know to be my ancient professed enemy, I no sooner received this message by him than I rightly conceived your meaning; and if, as you say, confessing a truth indeed may procure my safety, I shall with all willingness and duty perform your command. But do not imagine that your poor wife will ever confess a fault which she never even imagined. Never had prince a more dutiful wife than you have in Anne Boleyn, with which name and place I could willingly have contented myself if God and your Grace's pleasure had so been pleased. Nor did I ever so far forget myself in my exaltation but that I always looked for such an alteration as now; my preferment being only grounded on your Grace's fancy. You chose me from a low estate, and I beg you not to let an unworthy stain of disloyalty blot me and the infant Princess your daughter. Let me have a lawful trial, and let not my enemies be my judges. Let it be an open trial, I fear no open shames, and you will see my innocency cleared or my guilt openly proved; in which case you are at liberty both to punish me as an unfaithful wife, and to follow your affection, already settled on that party for whose sake I am now as I am, whose name I could somewhile since have pointed unto, your Grace being not ignorant of my suspicion therein. But if you have already determined that my death and an infamous slander will bring you the enjoyment of your desired happiness, then I pray God he will pardon your great sin, and my enemies, the instruments thereof. My innocence will be known at the Day of Judgment. My last request is that I alone may bear the burden of your displeasure, and not those poor gentlemen, who, I understand, are likewise imprisoned for my sake. If ever I have found favour in your sight, if ever the name of Anne Boleyn has been pleasing in your ears, let me obtain this request, and so I will leave to trouble your Grace any further.

From my doleful prison in the Tower.[12]

Anne asked for a lawful trial but it was a sham. She pleaded not guilty to all the charges laid against her but it was a done deal. Henry wanted the woman gone and once he had made his mind up, as he had done with Katherine, no one stood in his way.

Anne's uncle, the Duke of Norfolk, read out the verdict.

Because thou has offended our sovereign the King's grace in committing treason against his person and here attainted of the same, the law of the realm is this, thou hast deserved death, and thy judgement is this: that thou shalt be burned here within the Tower of London, on the Green, else to have thy head smitten off, as the King's pleasure shall be further known of the same.[13]

Five men had been charged with adultery with the queen: Mark Smeaton, Henry Norris, Sir Francis Weston, William Brereton and George, Lord Rochford – her brother. Only Smeaton confessed and probably only because he was tortured. Norris had never admitted to any adultery but he was charged with being solicited by the queen at Westminster on 6 October 1533, of adultery on 12 October, and at Greenwich in November. All dates that we now know were improbable. Norris had been particularly close to the king and the only thing he could be blamed for – if true – was a reported conversation he had had with Anne when she said Norris was waiting to fill dead men's shoes because he paid her the most attention and hadn't yet married his lover Margaret (Madge) Shelton, who is also thought to have been the king's mistress. Norris is supposed to have replied: 'if he should have any such thought, he would his head were off'. Words that were prophetic in the extreme. Sir Henry Norris along with Mark Smeaton, Sir Francis Weston, Sir William Brereton and Lord Rochford, were executed on 17 May.

Anne Boleyn was led to the scaffold on the morning of 19 May in front of a crowd of 1,000 people. She was beheaded with a single stroke of a French executioner's sword. Chapuys, who had hated the woman and referred to her as the concubine, at least was more complimentary at her demise commenting 'no one ever shewed more courage or greater readiness to meet death than she did'. On the same day, Cranmer issued a dispensation for Henry to marry Jane Seymour. It was Bryan, completely absolved of any wrongdoing, who was 'sent in all haste' to tell Jane Seymour the news. On 30 May at Whitehall Jane Seymour married Henry and was proclaimed queen on 4 June.

Husee had kept up with the news but told his master 'here are so many tales I cannot well tell which to write',[14] and in fact it was dangerous to write anything other than the official version of events. Lisle also received a response for Sir John Russell about his plea 'for something … by reason of these gentlemen's deaths', but the king had deemed that 'all things that were worthy of you were given before he received your letters'.[15] Husee had more information, saying that all things had been disposed and that there was nothing left worthy of Lisle except 'certain offices in Wales',[16] though the king thought that 'they were not fit for your lordship'.

Interestingly, it was Honor who wanted more information on Anne's downfall and she wrote several letters to Husee asking who had accused her. St Clare Byrne posited that Husee's response was the only contemporary document that mentioned names, and he states 'what was said was wondrous discreetly spoken: the first accusers, the Lady Worcester, and Nan Cobham and one maid more'.[17] Lady Worcester was the sister of Sir Anthony Browne and half-sister to Sir William Fitzwilliam; Nan Cobham was probably Anne Braye, Countess of Cobham and a member of the queen's household. The one maid more is thought to refer to Margery Horsman.

This year saw not only the deaths of two queens but also the start of the dissolution of the monasteries. Over 800 monasteries were dissolved displacing around some 12,000 monks, canons, friars and nuns. Henry VIII as Supreme Head of the Church of England now had the authority to disband monasteries across the country and seize their property and assets. Many people blame Cromwell for his role in the dissolution of the monasteries, but apart from the king absolutely supporting the destruction it was actually Wolsey who made the first foray into cashing in on religious orders. He dissolved twenty-nine monasteries between 1524 and 1527, including Bayham Abbey, Felixstowe Priory, Lesnes Abbey and Ravenstone Priory, raising around £1,800 to finance the building of his school in Ipswich and Cardinal's College in Oxford.

Of course Cromwell was Wolsey's man, which may have given him the idea to raise money for the crown by suppressing further monasteries but there is evidence that he was not comfortable with the wholesale destruction of religious orders. He was, however, a talented administrator and Henry would use him to carry out his plans making him Vicegerent of Spirituals in 1535 to act on his behalf. The court of augmentations would also be set up to manage the transfer of monastic properties and revenues.

In 1536 an act was passed for the dissolution of the minor monasteries, which were those with an income of less than £200 a year. The act stated that:

> the manifest sin, vicious carnal and abominable living is daily used and committed among the little and small abbeys, priories and other religious houses of monks canons and nuns where the congregation of such religious persons is under the number of 12 persons.[18]

Visiting commissioners had been travelling the country assessing the monasteries and in some cases falsely reporting back scandals, financial offences and sexual transgressions. Cromwell gave them orders to ask eighty-six questions including things like: Whether the divine service was kept up, day and night, in the right hours? Whether they (monks) kept company with women, within or without the monastery? Whether they had any boys lying by them?

The crown, of course, gained financially by selling off of monastic property and land to the nobles, albeit at cheap prices. It has been suggested that this is exactly why the upper echelons of Tudor society supported the dissolution as it added to their land portfolios. Another point that has been made is that this grab for land was also a defensive mechanism. If a noble had lands surrounding a monastery they needed to also own it so that a stranger and/or enemy didn't end up with property within their own holdings.

Lord Lisle's mention of wanting one such property is the first we find in any Tudor correspondence that the dissolution was happening. Lisle had in mind Beaulieu Abbey in Hampshire, but Husee thought it already granted and suggested he look at other properties like St Mary's in Winchester or Waverley in Surrey. Beaulieu would eventually go to Thomas Wriothesley, 1st Earl of Southampton, who would pay £1,350 for the privilege of owning it and allow the abbey to fall into ruin while he built his own home there. Lisle would have to wait some time for his own gain of the spoils.

Calais was on alert from 17 June as war was declared at Boulogne between Francis I and Charles V. The hostilities would continue for the next two years and although England was neutral Lisle had to monitor what was happening close to the Pale. Most of the fighting would occur in Italy, but Charles V invaded Provence and took Aix in August 1536. He was stopped by the French army before he reached Marseilles and any immediate threat to Calais was neutralised.

Still, their defences needed to be readied. One issue that was resolved this year was that of Wingfield's Marsh. Finally the Council of Calais received word that the king approved the drowning of the marsh so that this area would be underwater and impassable. The work had already started but must not have been complete as they were informed that they 'should do it without rancour or malice', and also that they 'should have a respect to the preservation of the haven'.[19] It would be confirmed by an act of parliament.

Although there was much to be done in Calais, Lisle was still looking for a licence to travel to England. Now that Sir Henry Norris was no longer in the picture, Husee had attempted to deal with John Heneage and Sir John Russell; he did not think much of them, although they had promised to talk to Cromwell on Lisle's behalf. He told Lisle 'I like none of these coloured dilations, with sweet words and little deeds.'[20] Lisle had lost an invaluable supporter in Norris and now he had few men at court to speak for him. Husee thought: 'If your friends were now as earnest in your suits to the King as Mr Norris was, your matters had not slept so long.'[21]

Husee was wise and a good counsellor in so many ways. He knew of his master's financial struggles and had trouble gaining credit for him but he felt that Lisle really needed to see the king in person to discuss his debts, including his payments to Edward Seymour. The king was planning to go to Dover once more and Husee was pressing for Lisle's licence.

While he waited he heard that Cromwell had been made Lord Privy Seal and days later, Baron Cromwell of Wimbledon. Lisle's letters to Cromwell are missing for this time but a response given by Cromwell on 10 July points to some souring of their relationship. Cromwell wrote:

I have received your letters and perceive as well as by the same as by other report that ye should take unkindly my letters lately sent unto you, taking thereby occasion to judge me to be displeased with you. I assure your lordship, howsoever I wrote I meant no ill.[22]

Cromwell mentions 'by other report' – was someone else stirring the waters?

Husee was put off time and again for Lisle's licence, but on 18 July he was instructed all was in order and he was expected at Dover on the 22nd. In this same correspondence came the news that Henry's illegitimate son, Henry Fitzroy, Duke of Richmond, who had once visited Lisle in Calais, was very sick. He would die five days later, possibly of consumption, at St James's Palace.

Lisle and Honor duly travelled to Dover and received an audience with Henry and Queen Jane. What passed between uncle and nephew we do not know but Lisle came away with the promise of a gift of monastic property to the value of one hundred marks. Such a gift shows that Henry was pleased with his uncle and his short trip was lengthened when Henry asked both himself and Honor to accompany the court on to Canterbury.

Honor suggested Frithelstock Priory, close to Umberleigh in Devon, might be a suitable property as their gift from the king and Husee would now be caught up in months of negotiation with the chancellor of the new Court of Augmentations, Sir Richard Riche, with whom Husee found 'very small friendship'.[23] Riche had once worked for Wolsey and had become Solicitor General before taking up his post of Chancellor of the Court of Augmentations in April 1536. The king had promised Lisle that his grant would include inheritance rights – a special mark of his esteem – but Husee would find Riche 'full of dissimulation' when it came to getting the paperwork signed and felt that 'he will deserve neither thanks ne reward'.[24] As the situation continued Husee began to wonder if the priory would even be worth the trouble of getting. Riche told him that it would be stripped of the leads on the roof as the king wished to cash in on this part of all the dissolved monasteries. Sir George Carew had also been given a twenty-one year lease on some of the property so Lisle would receive a rent from him but not be able to do anything with the priory and its lands and, to top it all, Husee did not think that Riche would allow Lisle inheritance rights. Husee's plan was to get Cromwell on side and if not him, the king himself. He absolutely foresaw the battle ahead.

Lisle received a letter from Henry in August but it had nothing to do with his grant – Henry did not trouble himself with these matters when he had competent administrators around him. Instead, due to the ongoing hostilities between France and the Holy Roman Emperor, the king wanted to ensure Calais was victualled. After all the trouble Lisle had had in previous years getting supplies, now that Calais might be caught in a hostile environment, he had the king's approval to make sure the retinue were well fed and the town defensible so that 'you shall see all other things of defence put in such readiness as not sudden chance may happen of what sort soever it should be that might put you to any notable distress or danger to the peril of our said town and to our dishonour', but as Henry wrote Lisle also needed 'to foresee the statute and ordinance made for the gunners … as we be informed hath been hitherto neglected to our no little marvel'.[25]

Husee did so much for the Lisles and strived to make sure his suits were dealt with, as well as running errands for Lady Lisle and dealing with issues over their properties and land in England. He wrote regularly, updating them on his progress as well as sharing any news he picked up, but in October it appears that Lisle had not been as grateful as he should have been and Husee was upset, writing:

And now that I have touched all your lordship's causes as much as in me lieth, I can do no less but open unto the same my grieved stomach, which is, that your lordship should report and say that I have had more mind to make banquets and to ride about to my kinsfolk than to apply any of your causes and businesses, which grieveth me not a little. I am sure I have not exceeded in banquets; and to say that ever I came in any kinman's house of mine this xij month, I dare well justify the contrary, and scant to my brother's house in the town once a month. It sticketh not a little in my stomach and I have always thought your lordship would have been better lord unto me than to have thus reported.[26]

Poor Husee! We don't have Lisle's reply but surely he regretted his words. Husee may have been his servant, but he deserved a break at times and who would blame him for a decent meal and his family's company. There was some compensation for his service in October when he received a grant for life from the Crown as 'searcher of the lordships of Marke and Oye within the Calais pale', which came with an extra 8d a day on top of his garrison wages.

There comes a break now in Lisle's correspondence from England. He received only two letters from Husee at the beginning of October and his only elusion to what was happening was to write; 'Here hath been a busy world, I pray God amend it.'

By October, dissent in the North culminated in an uprising in Lincolnshire. The religious changes that Henry had enacted to allow his marriage to Anne, his break with Rome and the establishment of the new Church of England plus the dissolution of the monasteries, all added to the rebel's grievances. Up to 50,000 Catholic men from Louth and the surrounding Lincolnshire towns of Caistor, Grimbsy, Yarborough, Market Rasen and Horncastle marched on Lincoln and occupied Lincoln Cathedral. They demanded the right to worship as Catholics and that Lincolnshire churches would be protected from desecration.

The Lincolnshire rising had dissipated but now there was trouble in Yorkshire. Robert Aske, a London barrister originally from Richmond, North Yorkshire, led his growing band of men to York. The rebellion was known as the Pilgrimage of Grace and was the largest and most severe Henry had ever faced during his reign. Aske, with his followers, wanted the dissolution of the monasteries to stop and England to return to Rome. Theirs were religious grievances, but there were also political and economic factors: poor harvests, unwelcome taxes, the loss of Katherine as queen, and the rise of the much-disliked Thomas Cromwell, the king's secretary and chancellor. It was not the king they blamed as such, but men like Cromwell whose evil policies had changed the country. The rebels sought change and were well organised. Their banner was of Christ's five wounds and they all took an oath to their cause.

Ye shall not enter into this our Pilgrimage of Grace
for the commonwealth, but only for the love that ye do bear
unto Almighty God his faith, and to Holy Church militant
and the maintenance thereof;
to the preservation of the King's person and his issue,
to the purifying of the nobility,
and to expulse all villein blood and evil councillors
against the commonwealth
from his Grace and his Privy Council of the same.
And that ye shall not enter into our said Pilgrimage

for no particular profit to yourself,
nor to do any displeasure to any private person,
but by counsel of the commonwealth,
nor slay nor murder for no envy,
but in your hearts put away all fear and dread,
and take afore you the Cross of Christ,
and in your hearts His faith,
the restitution of the Church,
the suppression of these heretics and their opinions,
by all the holy contents of this book.[27]

Robert Aske and his rebels took York and laid siege to Pontefract Castle. Its guardian Lord Darcy had informed Henry of their precarious position as the rebel troops amassed around them, telling him that they were in great danger of their lives and could see no way out of the situation. Darcy surrendered along with the castle inhabitants on 21 October and took the Pilgrims' oath. Henry was not impressed.

The Duke of Norfolk and the Earl of Shrewsbury were sent by the king to meet with over 30,000 agitators near Doncaster. The king's army was vastly outnumbered and to avoid the potential for mass slaughter, Norfolk promised the crowd that all would be pardoned if they dispersed. Aske agreed, if the king would address their demands, including that a parliament should be held at York or Nottingham, that the Princess Mary should be declared legitimate, suppressed monasteries be restored to their former state, Papal authority re-established and Cromwell removed from power and a truce was issued for the king to consider the rebel's proposals. Henry received their demands but asked for time to consider them. He was playing for time in the hope the rebellion would disband. He suggested they write down a more detailed description of their demands clarifying their position so that they could be addressed. For now an unsettled peace would ensue.

Lisle had had scant news about the Northern uprising and it must have seemed like he was a world away. He had some news of his own – Honor was expecting their first child. Husee had been one of the first people Honor told and he soon broadcast it to all who would listen. It was not long before letters of congratulation came flooding in.

One from Sir John Wallop was accompanied by some waters that would help 'when a woman's breasts be long, it raiseth them higher and rounder, which, peradventure shall be good for some of your neighbours!' but he hastened to add that, 'As for my Lady, needeth not.'[28]

But Husee had done something to upset his mistress and had heard rumours to that effect. Perhaps he had spread the news of her pregnancy too early, but again he was sick with the thought of the Lisles' displeasure and he told Honor, 'it was not a little grief unto my stomach. I think I was born in an unfortunate hour.'[29] However, he took a firmer tone with Lisle in December when he heard he was displeased with him for writing no news. Either Husee was super sensitive or Lisle was too demanding, or a mixture of both, but Husee this time had a warning to give:

> I spake with one that came from your lordship, who told me that your lordship is displeased with me because I write no news. I have written your lordship in my former letters the danger thereof, trusting that your lordship will be therewith pleased; for if I should write it might chance that I thereby might put myself in danger of my life and also put your lordship to displeasure, for there is divers here that hath been punished for reading and copying with publishing abroad of news; yea, some of them are at this hour in the Tower and like to suffer therefor.[30]

He was referring to Sir George Throckmorton and Sir William Essex. Both of these men were loyal to the king and had raised troops to fight the Lincolnshire rebels but they had indeed inadvertently played with fire.

Sir George Throckmorton was given a copy of 'Aske's Manifesto', seemingly unaware it was a banned publication. He lent it to Essex who made a copy before returning it. But someone else had also copied it – a chamber boy in Essex's household, who had lent it to the landlord of the Cardinal Inn in Reading, who also made a copy and on it went until Reading was awash with copies of the banned manifesto. When Throckmorton realised the danger he was in he burnt his copy, but it was too late. Under examination he protested that there were copies everywhere and it was probably the truth as, after a spell in the Tower, both Throckmorton and Essex, plus the chamber boy, were released.

Lisle was anxious to hear what was happening in the North but Husee was loath to put anything specific on paper especially after the Throckmorton affair. He wrote generally, for example, 'the Northern men hath obeyed the King's proclamation',[31] or that the news was 'all good, and all things well ended'.[32] He was showing caution in a dangerous time, but Lisle continued to moan about Husee's work and the lack of progress in his suits. If he had been at court perhaps he would have been more aware of the seriousness of the rebellion in the North.

On 6 December the Duke of Norfolk was presented with the pilgrims' '24 articles' at Doncaster. In it the rebels asked for a general pardon, religious reform, that parliament would be held in York or Nottingham, that the Lady Mary be made legitimate, and that 'Lord Cromwell, the Lord Chancellor, and Sir Ric. Riche to have condign punishment, as subverters of the good laws of the realm and maintainers and inventors of heretics.'[33] Norfolk agreed to the parliament at York and a pardon for those involved in the rebellion. The other matters would be passed to the king. Aske, being happy that Henry had listened to their demands and change would occur, disbanded the rebel army. For now the threat of rebellion was over and Aske would be invited to spend Christmas with the court at Greenwich. Henry would use his charms to woo Aske and make him believe he was on his side, but the king had other ideas and the following year would put them into practice.

Husee had to constantly assure Lisle that he was doing all he could for him. With the rebellion, the men he had to deal with at court were all caught up in other issues. Cromwell had been hard to see, the Court of Augmentations was a nightmare and Husee's agenda was full. We can imagine him having to wait hours for a few moments' discussion, being utterly frustrated by not getting clear answers for his master and trying his best to gain support for his master's causes.

Richard Lee, Surveyor of Calais, at least let Lisle know that he was working with Husee to talk to Cromwell about Frithelstock Priory. Regardless of the act now detailing how rooms should be given to retinue members, Lee had been proffered over William Pole, who was 'not well pleased' he had been passed over, but it was obvious that Lisle had to place Lee in the retinue due to his position and, in thanks, Lee was helping Lisle's causes while he was in England. In the same letter he also describes the procession of the king and queen from Westminster to Greenwich for Christmas.

The King's Majesty and the Queen, with all dukes, lords and the ambassadors of the Emperor rode through the City of London, whereas they were received so honourably as the like sight hath not been seen here since the Emperor's being here: the streets hanged about with arras and cloth of gold, priests in their copes with their crosses and censers on the one side and the citizens of London, every man in his degree, on the other side. It rejoiced every man wondrously.[34]

Such news made Lisle homesick and even more eager to return to England.

Chapter Seven

The Problem of Pole
1537

Husee presented Lisle's gift to the king at New Year as was his annual custom. This year he managed to speak a few words with the king on Lisle's behalf and told him how pleased his master had been to see him at Dover. He also told him the pregnant Honor was doing well and the king hoped that they would have a son as Lisle would then be 'a joyful father, and said further that your lordship had the gentlest heart living',[1] and sent his regards.

Husee was also first with the news that Robert Aske left London on his return to Yorkshire on 5 January 'with most haste, but what the matter is God knoweth; for all things are kept secret'.[2] At the same time, another rebellion broke out in Cumberland and Westmorland. Sir Francis Bigod, who had served Cardinal Wolsey, led the rebellion which Robert Aske tried to stop, telling the rebels that they put their pardon from the king at risk. Henry didn't care that he had won Aske over and now he had every reason to accuse them all of treason.

The Duke of Norfolk was ordered to end the rebellion in the North once and for all. He was given carte blanche for revenge. 'You must cause such dreadful execution upon a good number of the inhabitants, hanging them on trees, quartering them, and setting their heads and quarters in every town, as shall be a fearful warning.'[3] Many were executed, others were sent to London for trial, Aske included. Aske would be convicted of high treason in Westminster and taken back to York for his execution.

There was trouble in Calais too, when twenty or thirty men of war entered the Pale to search for Burgundians supposedly under the command of Lisle's correspondent Captain du Bies. Lisle had ordered the roundup of certain strangers in the town and seen them safely escorted on their way to avoid any trouble. He informed Cromwell, but Sir Richard Grenville had also told him of his concern over the amount of strangers in the town and marches that could be made citizens. He felt there were hundreds, with their wives and children who 'without controlment, shall by day go upon the walls of the town and all hours in the night abouts in the streets'. He was concerned for the safety of Calais and worried 'what shall come of it God knoweth'.[4] The daily raids into the Pale would continue.

And the retinue were not happy, having not been paid their wages again. The money that should have found its way to Calais had been needed to fund the army that was sent north to quell the rebellion. There had also been an issue with the licences Lisle was signing for members of the retinue to take leave. Husee took a stern tone when he told his master:

I have seen passports which your lordship hath signed and sealed, wherein is written 'as you tender our pleasure', reciting the same words over 2 or 3 times, which I think passed your lordship unaware; but surely he that writ them wist not well what he did, for though your lordship meant no hurt, it might chance, if it come to some men's hands or sight, they would scan the same to the worst. It shall be requisite, after my poor judgement, that your lordship peruse them better from henceforwards[5]

Lisle took Husee's advice and recalled recently given licences and amended their wording. But this was proof that sometimes Lisle was lax in his duties and that others noticed. Lisle was known to easily sign documents in front of him without perusing their contents, and the ease with which he signed licences to travel would rear its head again in 1540.

Reginald Pole was made Cardinal by the Pope in December 1536. Reginald Pole was the son of Sir Richard Pole, who had been chamberlain to Prince Arthur, and Margaret Plantagenet, Countess of Salisbury, and the grandson of Edward IV's younger brother, George, 1st Duke of Clarence. As such he was Lisle's kinsman, the child of his cousin Margaret, although they do not appear to have corresponded and did not have a close relationship. Pole had asked the Pope to defer his nomination to Cardinal in fear of endangering his family, for he knew he had angered Henry VIII, as did others. In a letter to Lisle Sir John Wallop says: 'I am right sorry, for I know well the King cannot take it well'.[6]

Pole had been supported in his career in the church by the king, who had also paid for his education. He left England in 1532 to continue his theological studies in Italy but angered the king while he was there by writing *Pro ecclesiasticae unitatis defensione* (Defence of the Unity of the Church), which refuted Henry's supremacy and urged him to return to the Catholic Church and the Pope's authority. The newly ordained Cardinal had initially supported Henry in his divorce, but when Henry asked for his support in confirming that marrying his dead brother's wife had been wrong, *Pro ecclesiasticae unitatis defensione* was Pole's response, in which he lambasted Henry in the strongest terms:

> You have squandered a huge treasure; you have made a laughing stock of the nobility; you have never loved the people; you have pestered and robbed the clergy in every possible way; and lately you have destroyed the best men in your kingdom, not like a human being, but a wild beast.[7]

He also declared that his mother's brother, his uncle Warwick, was innocent and urged Charles V to invade England. Pole put down in words what many people were thinking but were too scared to say.

His mother Margaret was forced to say that 'she took her said son for a traitor and for no son, and that she would never take him otherwise'.[8] Henry could reach the Pole family in England, whereas Reginald was far from his grasp – but it would have devastating results. For now the king made Pole's family write to him. Margaret wrote:

> Son Reginald, I send you God's blessing and mine, though my trust to have comfort in you has turned to sorrow. Alas that I, for your folly, should receive from my sovereign lord such message as I have late done by your brother, to me as a woman, his Highness has shown such mercy and pity as I could never deserve, but that I trusted my children's services would express my duty. And now, to see you in his Grace's indignation, – trust me, Reginald, there went never the death of thy father or of any child so nigh my heart. Upon my blessing I charge thee to take another way and serve our master, as thy duty is, unless thou wilt be the confusion of thy mother. You write of a promise made by you to God, – Son, that was to serve God

and thy prince, whom if thou do not serve with all thy wit, with all thy power, I know thou can not please God. For who hath brought you up and maintained you to learning but his Highness? Will pray God to give him grace to serve his prince truly or else to take him to his mercy.[9]

Henry, Lord Montagu, his older brother, also wrote but in stronger terms:

I perceive by your letter of 15 July that you remember the unkindness I reckoned in you when your sentence was required in the King's matter, and that now you fear I would take more displeasure. I knew nothing of the effect of your book when I received your letter, which made me greatly to doubt what before I had hoped for. To be out of doubt, spoke with the Lord Privy Seal, to whom you are as much bound as if you were his near kinsman. He advised me to speak with the King, but said nothing himself. At time convenient spoke with the King, who declared a great part of your book so at length that it made my poor heart so to lament that if I had lost mother, wife, and children it could no more have done, for that had been but natural. But you, to show yourself so unnatural to so noble a prince, of whom you cannot deny next God you have received all things. And for our family, which was clean trodden under foot, he set up nobly, which showeth his charity, his clemency, and his mercy.

I grieve to see the day that you should set forth the contrary, or trust to your wit above the rest of the country, whose mind you will perceive from him whom you bade read your book. If there is any grace in you, now you will turn to the right way, and then we may reckon it was the will of God that your ingratitude should show the King's meekness. He has borne your slanders more patiently than the poorest in the country could do, and is contented that your friends should instruct you of what moves them, as I know those who are learned have done. I, who lack learning, could never conceive that laws made by man were of such strength but that they might be undone again by man, for what seems politic at one time, by abusion proves at another time the contrary. Therefore, gentle Reginald, let no scrupulosity so embrace your stomach but that we, which be so knit in nature and so happily born under so noble a prince, may so join together to serve him, as our bounden duties requireth. It is incredible to me that by reason of a brief sent to you from the bishop of Rome you should be resident with him this winter. If you should take that way, then fare well all my hope. Learning you may well have, but doubtless no prudence nor pity, but showeth yourself to run from one mischief to another. And then farewell all bonds of nature, not only of me, but of all mine, or else instead of my blessing they shall have my curse. But utterly out of hope I cannot be that ever superstition should so reign in you that you would so highly offend God to lose the benefits of so noble a prince, your native country, and whole family, without the devil have so much power over you, from the which to keep you I shall as heartily pray, as I would be partner of the joys of Heaven, which Christ make us partakers of.[10]

Reginald Pole would later comment that the king knew well how much he loved his family 'and tried to use them to sway me by writing letters which accused me of renouncing my king. Told them I had another and that if I lost them, would have the love of the martyrs'.[11]

The Pope had wanted Pole to visit the Northern rebels and lend his support, but his departure had been delayed and as we know the rebellion was suppressed. Henry was taking no chances with his errant kinsman. Not many people knew of his publication and the king wanted to keep it that way, even though the Cardinal had no intention of making his work public. Pole was currently travelling across Europe and in April Sir Francis Bryan was sent to France to ask Francis I for the arrest and extradition of Cardinal Reginald Pole.

Pole had been informed when he reached the court at Paris that he was unwelcome and should leave. The Cardinal was also turned away from Brussels before seeking sanctuary at Cambrai, neutral territory controlled by the Cardinal Bishop of Liege. Bryan had missed him in Paris and lost the chance of having him imprisoned.

On 21 April, the bishop of Faenza, papal nuncio in France, was reporting:

Brian, the new English ambassador, who being a favourite of that King never comes here for anything [not?] very important, came to make a last effort to get the Legate into his hands and bring him into England, into the catalogue of the other martyrs. Not having succeeded, he is very desperate, and as discontent as possible with the French, and brags, saying that if he found him [the Legate] in the midst of France he would kill him with his own hand, and similar big words. This shows clearly the mind of that King, and how necessary it is that the Legate should take care of his life, having to deal with fools and wretches, and that they fear [him] more, as I gather from him [the Legate], than anything else from Rome.[12]

What others had realised was that Bryan was on a mission to see Pole dead and Henry said as much when he wrote to his ambassadors:

And for as much as we would be very glad to have the said Pole by some mean trussed up and conveyed to Calais, we desire and pray you to consult and devise between you there-upon. If they think it feasible, Brian shall secretly appoint fellows for the purpose.[13]

And the person Bryan had chosen was Sir Thomas Palmer, Knight Porter of Calais. In a letter, Cromwell suggested that he had been chosen to apprehend and possibly kill Pole, and Palmer had been sent the sum of £100 for the purpose. Lisle certainly knew that Palmer was involved in apprehending Pole, as Palmer wrote to him from Cambrai that the Cardinal 'did not come out of his lodging, nor intends not'.[14] How did Lisle feel about this attempt to destroy his kinsman? If he felt any internal wrangling, he was first and foremost loyal to the king.

Pole anyway evaded all capture and Henry had to reign in the attempt:

Touching your further proceeding for the apprehension of his traitor Pole … his Highness perceiving by the rest of your letters that his intent therein is so disclosed, or at least suspected, that being the said Pole thereupon advertised, as ye write he is, to take heed of the preservation of himself, there is no likelihood there ye should be able to conduce that matter to his desire, his Majesty mindeth not to advance any money for his said apprehension.[15]

Presumably Sir Palmer returned to his position at Calais and Cardinal Pole returned to Rome. Henry would never be able to get his revenge on him – his family, however, would be another matter.

Bryan visited Lisle when he stopped at Calais on his way home. Husee reported from London in April that the king had been troubled by his leg (a suppurating ulcer that would never heal) and seldom went out. He assured Lisle that:

It were good your Lordship did speak earnestly unto Mr Bryan at his return, and make him your friend in all such things as your Lordship shall have ado here at the Court; for surely, if he set in his foot with his good mind, he hath no fellow now in the Privy Chamber.[16]

Bryan would be a good friend and 'stick to' Lisle.

Honor's pregnancy was progressing and at the beginning of May Husee beat any official news by telling Lisle that Queen Jane was pregnant too – a fact that would not be made public until 27 May. He was delighted with the news saying: 'I pray Jesu send us a prince, which would make all England merry!'[17] Perhaps then the king's mood would improve. Queen Jane had a craving for fat quails and since none were to be found in England, Lisle was asked to send some over from France. Honor made sure they were dispatched regularly, hoping they would gain her favour with the queen.

In the past Honor had tried to place her daughters Anne and Katherine in service to Queen Anne. Now Honor was trying to get her daughters a place in the new queen's household and had asked Margaret, Countess of Salisbury, (and Lisle's cousin) to help her. Margaret had had a long court career as governess of the Princess Mary from May 1520 until July 1521 and again from 1525 to 1533. Mary referred to her as her second mother and Margaret was absolutely devoted to her charge. When Henry disbanded his daughter's household in 1533, Margaret 'offered to follow and serve her at her own expense, with an honourable train'.[18]

Henry rudely referred to Margaret at this time as 'a fool, of no experience', and thought she was a bad influence on his daughter, but Chapuys saw her as Lady Mary's protector and with her there to look after her:

They would no longer be able to execute their bad designs, which are evidently either to cause her to die of grief or in some other way, or else to compel her to renounce her rights, marry some low fellow, or fall prey to lust, so that they may have a pretext and excuse for disinheriting her.[19]

Being forced to stay away from the princess, Margaret collapsed and it was her son Lord Montagu who wrote to Honor with the news 'My lady my mother lies at Bisham, to whom I made your ladyship's recommendations. I assure you she is very weak, but it is to her great comfort to hear of my lord and your ladyship'.[20]

After this Margaret appeared rarely at court. Nevertheless, she put in a good word with Queen Jane and advised Honor to make sure her daughter attended the queen's coronation – although Henry's third queen would never be crowned. Lisle rarely heard from his cousin Margaret but had kept up a correspondence with her oldest son Henry, Lord Montagu, who signed his letters 'your loving cousin', and assured Lisle that 'of no kinsman he hath he shall be more assured of to do him pleasure'.[21] Lisle in turn allowed him the use of his house at Soberton and he wrote to him after Honor had approached him as well to ask for his support. Montagu replied:

> my lady your bedfellow writ to me to speak to my lady my mother for a daughter of hers, in which you may be both assured I will do that may be in me. But and it please you to write a letter to my lady my mother yourself it will sooner take effect.[22]

Whether Lisle contacted his cousin to further Anne's career, we do not know. Honor had also asked Eleanor Paston, the Countess of Rutland, Mary Arundell and Margery Horsman to help and was rewarded when, through their auspices, Queen Jane sent for both of the girls saying she would choose the one she liked best. Anne, who may later have become one of the king's mistresses, was asked to serve the queen while Katherine joined the Countess of Rutland's household.

Lord Sandys had arrived at Guisnes in March. Although he was captain of a fortified town in the Pale he tended to only take up his position in the summer months, spending six months in France and returning to England for the winter. Lisle had entertained him en route in Calais. As Sandys pointed out, they needed to work together as their roles had 'one purpose, without making contrary or divisions in them, seeing the one must of reason and force be assistant to the other'.[23] The tone of his letters shows some disparity between them, perhaps with Lisle asserting his higher station, as Sandys often refers to Lisle's governance and authority before trying to establish they are also equals as in this paragraph:

> I trust you will that as your poor friend, and one appointed by the Council of this county, I may, when poor men dwelling within my rule complain upon wrongs, write unto your lordship, in their favour of their right, and desire your goodness towards them, as I would your lordship in like case should command me, which as I take it is a corroboration unto your rules and governances.[24]

Some things that Sandys did resulted in appeals to Lisle, as in the case of Bastien Lambert who had been allowed to bring livestock and goods into the Pale for the past two years but had now been stopped by Sandys. The Lady of Landretun, Jenne de Quieret, asked Lisle to write to Sandys to allow the man and 'his little son' to be 'free of interference in your territory'.[25] Sandys regularly sent information about the movements of French or Imperial forces close to the Pale and made sure Cromwell was also informed, but Husee told his master it should be he who should 'procure ever the first news, although it were something the more to your cost and pains' so that he had 'the thanks and not my Lord Chamberlain'.[26] Lisle needed to be seen to be doing his job and doing it well, so that Sandys did not receive all the credit. As it was, hostilities between France and the Emperor would cease in August with a truce.

These were small appeals compared to, for instance, the issues over retinue rooms, and it is hard to say how much time Lisle gave to them. Come May he was caught up again, as Sir William Fitzwilliam put it, 'contrary to the new law lately made in the town of Calais, [you] admitted one into a gunner's room'.[27] Fitzwilliam wanted to know whether he intended to violate or break the new law and warned him he risked the king's displeasure. Lisle hadn't actually admitted anyone, but there was more potential here for gunner positions to cause problems. Gunnery practice was held twice a week for soldiers of the retinue and others to practice their skills. George Browne, Master of the Ordnance of Calais, oversaw the two-hour long sessions and was on the lookout for those who showed promise and who would rise from the rank of soldier to gunner.

It's possible that Browne and Lisle were at odds over who would get the next place and Fitzwilliam had heard of someone's preference contrary to the king's wishes.

There was an appeal from Cromwell in July for Lisle to support Lady Whethill, now a widow. If Lisle had thought with Sir Richard's death it would be an end to his dealings with their family, he was mistaken. Their son Robert, he who caused such a fuss over gaining a room in the retinue, had disputed his father's will.

For Lisle these were just minor irritations, but July of this year would see the beginning of a series of events that would culminate in his downfall. Calais was known as a hotbed of religious dissent full of 'gossip and slander and petty feuds',[28] and John Butler, Commissary of Calais, reported to Cranmer that there were two priests in the town who were 'great enemies of the truth'.[29] One of them, Sir William Minstreley, was imprisoned for his inflammatory ideas but the other, Sir William Richardson, who Butler felt should have been punished 'for using of sorcery and other things',[30] had escaped punishment so far with the help of Lady Lisle and others.

Cromwell ordered the Council to send the men over to England to be examined and sent a stern warning to the Council from the king who:

Willed me plainly to intimate unto you all and every of you, that in case he shall perceive from henceforth any such abuses suffered or winked at, as have been hitherto in manner in contempt of his most royal estate maintained, his Highness will put others in the best of your rooms that shall so offend him, by whom he shall be better served.

And he added a pointed remark about Honor.

It is thought against all reason that the prayers of women and their fond flickerings should move any of you to do that thing that should in any wise displease your prince and sovereign lord or offend his just laws.[31]

This warning to the Council was followed by a personal letter from Cromwell to Lisle. He reiterated that he knew some of the Council leaned towards the old religion, observations and rites, but assured Lisle he was still his 'perfect and sincere friend'.[32] He would help him with his suits when needed and all was well between them. At this stage there was no hint that Lisle had in any way acted incorrectly but rather the opposite, he was still a trusted and competent servant of the king. He had informed Cromwell of the situation and acted appropriately. Husee had had an audience with Cromwell and suggested he write to Lisle. Lisle had obviously taken the situation badly and Husee had told the secretary that unless his master received a 'loving letter', it might put him 'in some hazard of disease or peril' of his life.[33] This may seem a dramatic touch, but this would not be the first time that Lisle's mental health and wellbeing would be mentioned. Four years of being in Calais were taking their toll.

When Husee wrote to his master next he told him not to take things so earnestly and grievously and that 'howsoever the world goeth your lordship shall need to take no care, for the King's majesty loveth your lordship well'. He assured him 'the world is yours, and I trust shall be better than it ever was'.[34]

When Lisle then heard of a priest at Guisnes who had 'caused the image of St Anne to be borne about',[35] he instructed Lord Sandys to have the man escorted to Calais to be imprisoned. That Cromwell instructed Husee to tell Lisle that he was to punish any offending priests in Calais and not send them over to England shows the Lord Privy Seal trusted Lisle to carry out his role as Lord Deputy competently. But the fact that the message had gone through Lisle's man and not committed to paper also pointed to what some have seen as Cromwell's protection of reformers where their punishments in Calais may have been less severe than if sent to London. Lisle for his part made sure to inform Cromwell of every matter – perhaps he was being over cautious, but given his previous reprimands and his very real fear of displeasing the king and the anguish it caused him, his need to be careful was overriding.

In August Lord Edmund Howard, the king's comptroller in Calais, was elected as mayor by the burgesses and aldermen of Calais, but Lisle refused to swear him in. He pointed out that the mayor made his accounts to the comptroller and if Howard was both it would be very strange. There appears to be no love lost between the mayors, burgesses and aldermen and the Lord Deputy and the Council. Both Whethill and

Wingfield had been mayors and we have seen the issues that arose with their in-fighting. Lisle, now used to others going over his head, wrote to Cromwell pre-empting their outcry. But in this case Lisle was in the right and Husee informed him 'that the King's Majesty will in no wise that my Lord Howard be admitted unto the Mayoralty ... nor is he herewith pleased'.[36] Cromwell would be writing to the late mayor and aldermen to underline the king's and Lisle's decision.

Sandys was in support of Howard and we can see by the tone of his previous letters that he had no problem squaring up to Lisle, albeit in a manner of writing couched in courtesies. At the beginning of August Lisle had mistakenly opened a letter to Sandys and Lady Lisle had taken the trouble to forward it to him with her husband's apologies. Honor at times aided Lisle in his duties, especially where correspondence was concerned. Sandys was grateful but in his return letter, he makes sure Lisle knew not to do it again.

Notwithstanding, in time to come, when letters shall come unto your lordship directed unto me, I most heartily pray that I myself may first unclose them, and thereupon, as your goodness bindeth me, I will most gladly make your lordship participant of their contynew. But my lord, I would most gladly, as reason is, as to take the pain upon myself first to unclose them, and I pray your good lordship that from henceforth I may do so.[37]

Lisle had had the backing of his nephew over the new mayor fiasco and finally he received word that he was now lord of Frithelstock Priory. The king's gift shows that at this point he was still very much in favour. Husee had spent many hours working towards this but told Lisle that Cromwell had said he must never sell it or risk the king's displeasure. He urged his master to write to the secretary and the king to give his thanks, even though he had assured them Lisle 'would not part from it for gold neither silver, considering it was the King's gift'.[38]

In the same letter Husee adds he has been looking after a seal that was a gift to the Lord Admiral from Lisle. He really did do everything and anything for his master! As none of the admiral's men would take the seal, Husee had kept her at Wapping for five weeks and paid for fish out of his own pocket to feed her, but she had refused to eat. Unfortunately there was no happy end for the poor creature. The Lord Admiral told Husee he had nowhere to keep it and to see that it was killed, baked and sent to his wife!

Sir Thomas Palmer had also been in London and at court and was received well by the king and Cromwell, but he was 'in a furore' at one meeting with the Lord Privy Seal who had sworn by God's blood they were all papists in Calais. Palmer had sworn back by God's heart they were not, and Cromwell had reluctantly admitted that did not include Palmer or Lisle. Palmer was desperate to return to Calais but was experiencing money difficulties and asked Lisle to write to have him sent home. He also told him that Cromwell had said 'that as long as the King's Grace doth live and he together, you shall remain King's Deputy at Calais, in despite of all will say contrary'.[39] Perhaps Lisle was becoming more concerned about his position – even though he wanted to return to England, he wanted to do so in favour – but this comment also shows he had his enemies at court. Palmer doesn't say who was saying contrary but there were obviously those that sought to undermine him.

On 12 October Queen Jane gave birth to Henry's longed-for son, Edward. Finally the king had his male heir that he had so longed for. Husee wrote how his birth 'rejoiced the realm'[40] more than anything had done in years. There was much celebrating and a resplendent christening in England, and at Calais shots were fired and thanksgiving prayers read out. But Henry's third wife was not to live to see her son grow up. Within days she died at Hampton Court palace, possibly of puerperal fever, and the king was plunged into the depths of despair.

For Honor and Lisle however, there was not to be such joyous news. She had been due to give birth in June and Husee's letters to her at the time often end with the note that he wished her a good delivery, but he was still sending this wish in July and at the beginning of August. By the end of August Husee had heard from Honor that things were not right. It seems she had been suffering a phantom pregnancy and he wrote to her such a consoling letter that it really shows how much the Lisles meant to him. He wrote:

Greatly to my discomfort to perceive and see that your ladyship should take such ways of lamentation and sorrows (and causeless), as my full trust in God is, for your ladyship is not the first woman

of honour that hath overshot or mistaken your time and reckoning
... for if it be his pleasure he spareth neither Empress, Queen,
Princess ne Duchess, but his handiwork must be suffered and his
mercy abiden...

Your ladyship can exhort and give others virtuous and good counsel,
and now should it best appear in your own person, which both by
your ladyship's writing and saying of others approveth for this time
contrary. For I have heard of divers that your ladyship weepeth and
sorroweth without comparison, which I assure your ladyship grieved
me no less than it were my own mother.[41]

Honor later would consult with a physician, Dr Le Coop, who diagnosed
her with 'cold and slemysh humours', which he told her could:

gather in the mother, where if they fortune to stick fast and congeal
together, there engendereth with also the blood that is retained a
swelling, even like as the woman conceived, and it doth move
himself neither more or less than if the child were conformed, which
deceiveth and abuseth many folks.[42]

It had been a phantom pregnancy and although extremely painful to bear,
there was nothing she could have done.

Lisle too felt the sadness and loss of what he had hoped would be
the birth of his heir and was suffering from depression, or 'motions of
melancholy' as Sir Thomas Palmer put it when he sent him a book that
he thought would help:

so that you may see that is good for the body is naught for the soul. I
think Jak off Rydyng hath a merrier life than either your lordship or
I have. I think that if I had not met with my book I had been stark
mad ere this time.[43]

Lisle had told Palmer that he would gladly leave Calais and Palmer did
not blame him. He was well aware of the Lord Deputy's struggles and of
life in Calais in general.

And still the problem of rooms was ongoing. Despite Palmer's reassurances of how the king and his Lord Privy Seal held him in high esteem, in November Lisle received a letter from Cromwell that raised the age old contentions over rooms for rent:

> I trust you consider what charge you have there under the King's majesty; and I would you should remember both what beseemeth a man to do, being in that place, and that the same containeth in it no state of inheritance ne term for life, but upon the good behaviour of the person having it. Now, if you should weigh the thing and nature of it indifferently, would you think it meet that a man should have that charge which would bring himself to such necessity that he should be constrained to put all things to sale that be committed upon special trust to his discretion, neglecting of the one part of the King's Highness honour to be sustained in the satisfaction of his grants, of the other part as it were contemning all friendship in giving place to a little lucre.[44]

Cromwell was right of course, in the sense that Lisle's position depended on the king, but despite the acts governing Calais, the problems persisted. Lisle had done his utmost to keep his superiors informed, to act with their permission and to maintain Calais and its retinue and remedy its issues, but he was only one man and he could do nothing to stop them from becoming progressively worse.

Chapter Eight

Feeling Forsaken
1538

As always, Lisle had instructed Husee to present the king with his new year's gift personally and Husee was delighted when the king troubled to talk to him, asking after Lisle and his wife and whether they were merry. There is such pride in Husee when he overhears Cromwell refer to him as Lord Lisle's man.

Although Husee had assured the king his uncle was well, he had in fact been suffering with a pain under his ribs. Husee had consulted one of the king's doctors, Walter Cromer, who would send on a remedy if the Lord Deputy detailed where exactly the pain was, but for now he had talked to a 'strange physician' who recommended powder of ginger 'for a wind under the left ribs'.[1]

At least it was nothing more serious. There was plague in England and Lisle was informed that the areas around Frithelstock Priory were badly affected. His man George Rolle had inspected Lisle's new property and seemed to think that he would be visiting soon, which was probably just wishful thinking on Lisle's part. Rolle was anxious that the great chamber had been ruined that winter 'by great winds and tempests',[2] although he felt the dorter (dormitory) and cloister might be made into lodgings.

As of yet Lisle had no permission to travel to England and he was caught up in the seizure of a French ship that had captured an English vessel. The French ship had been taken to Dartford and relieved of its crew. Henry wished to inspect it and agreed with William Fitzwilliam, Lord Admiral since the death of the Duke of Richmond, that Lisle could have the ship as long as he kept it ready should it be needed in service of the king. It would return to Calais as a patrol vessel but the Lord Deputy was not overly impressed with his 'gift' as it would mean paying for its upkeep and crew – another expense he could not afford. However several letters told him that his actions were much talked about and 'there is much honour spoken of you for that enterprise, at Court, of every man's mouth, to the great comfort of your lovers and friends in these parts'.[3] At least it improved his standing.

Around this time Lisle also heard from the wily but unlucky mariner Cheriton who was still trying to bring thirteen pieces of the king's ordnance back to home shores. Over the past two years he has been imprisoned, in debt, and his ship had been wrecked in foul weather. He was taken with Turkish slaves to Barbary and ransomed by the French Admiral for 250 crowns which he had to pay back and was now without funds, so he asked Lisle if he could help him out financially or else he would be 'undone for ever'.[4] It is such a shame we don't have Lisle's responses for the other side of the story. Given his own financial situation, it would be hard to believe he was ever able to help Cheriton out.

Husee had been asked by Lisle to obtain a licence so that he could once more go to England, and as usual he hastened to do his master's bidding and sought out Cromwell, but the Lord Privy Seal wanted to know 'what your lordship meant, and what you would do here'.[5] Husee told him that Lisle just wanted to see the king and open his mind and heart to him, but Cromwell was being cagey. Lisle threatened to go to court without permission and place himself at the king's mercy but Husee warned him 'you will in nowise do so, for there be many things incident towards displeasure in so attempting: for the town is of no small charge, and it is not to be doubted the King will foresee and well know in whose hands he put the custody thereof.'[6] If a licence could not be got now, Husee would do his best to gain one in the near future. We don't know what was so pressing at this time. Perhaps it was just that Lisle had been ill, was sorely tired of Calais and wanted to go home, but his permission to do so would not be yet forthcoming.

At least there was a family celebration to cheer them up. Lisle's eldest daughter Frances was married on 19 February to Honor's son, John Basset. Husee had been in England making preparations for the wedding and trying desperately to buy bridal clothes on credit even though he received no thanks for it. Writing to Honor to send his best wishes to the newly-weds, he added:

And where your ladyship writ that there was fault found because Mistress Frances' sleeves were not turned up with tinsel, and that her kirtle was not silver, I followed your ladyship's bill of proportion in it, for if your ladyship had written so to have had it it should not a'lacked.[7]

The religious issues that began to appear for Lisle in 1537 rose their head again this year. Husee wrote to Lady Lisle on 9 March with a warning 'to leave part of such ceremonies as you do use, as long prayers and offerings of candles, and at some time to refrain and not speak ... when you hear things spoken that liketh you not'.[8]

In conversation with Cromwell Husee had told him of the relics of Calais and when he showed him the sheep's tail relic 'he rejoiced not a little, and said that he was glad that your lordship had come to so good a point'.[9] However, he asked what Lady Lisle 'was' and when Husee said she was nothing like what had been reported, Cromwell told him she should be won over little by little. Who spoke against Honor and what they had said we cannot know, but it was obvious that her religious convictions were leading her on a dangerous path. This was not the first time Cromwell had shown some concern over Honor's religious leanings and it would not be the last. Husee was alert to any rumours concerning his mistress and wrote to her again at the end of March 'to leave the most part of your memories, and have only mass, matins, and evensong of the day'.[10] Two men were about to arrive in Calais that April who would have disastrous implications for Lisle and Honor. One Clement Philpot, the son of Sir Peter Philpot, was to join Lisle's household (and possibly be a match for their daughter Philippa) and also a 'sober and honest' priest, Sir Gregory Botolf. But their story will not play out just yet.

Edmund Howard, still hanging on to his position of comptroller but not mayor, wrote from London he was waiting to be sent back to Calais and when that happened Lisle would receive permission to travel to England. Husee was trying to get his master's licence to travel and Lisle told him he was in despair and could neither eat, drink or sleep until he had it. Yet again he complained to Husee that he was too slow in carrying out his orders and had not been writing to him of his progress often enough. Husee defended himself, with the patience of a saint, telling Lisle that 'I think that I have written always as time and opportunity served me; for I cannot attend upon the tide hourly, for sometime one hour missing attendance upon my Lord Privy Seal may hinder a month's suit.' He also pointed out he thought it pointless to write if he had nothing to say, but, and we can almost hear his sigh, he would write more often 'though the cause be ever so small'.[11]

Lisle was increasingly anxious to be received at court and talk to the king. He talked to Husee of 'back friends' – those that were slandering him – to which Husee reassured him 'their malice will not prevail where your person is present'.[12] But he was not present and he was increasingly unhappy when he still had not received licence to travel by May. Husee managed to see Cromwell and told him that his master felt that either he or the king were displeased with him and that's why he was not allowed to come to court. Lisle had heard that these back friends were talking about why he was not called to court and stories were spreading about him. Cromwell told Husee to inform Lisle that he should not take it badly, there had been other 'divers weighty causes and considerations' that had postponed his licence and that 'it should not be requisite that every mean personage should invent or imagine why, wherefore, or for what cause the stay was that you came not'.[13] He would be given permission to travel, but not yet.

As we have said, religion was in turmoil in England. Henry's break with Rome had not made it clear to the common people what was and was not permitted. There were grey areas and Lisle, as deputy, was as unsure himself. Lisle also was very loathe to do anything without the king's and Cromwell's permission and here we see the start of Lisle asking for clarification on religious matters and not getting it. As he mentions several times, he is not learned in such theological matters and needed advice.

In July Lisle wrote to the Lord Privy Seal and mentioned his previous letters had gone unanswered. There were several things to be broached; there were people in the town declaring 'divers things against the sacrament of the altar', a priest who had preached 'against the words of the King's book', and the general feeling across Europe that they were all heretics in Calais, 'out of the league with the Emperor and the French King, and that they trust to have war with us'.[14]

Cromwell did reply after two weeks and it is interesting to note that he starts his letter by saying he had actually received Lisle's sundry letters. So why had he delayed in responding to him? Was he really trying to protect Calais reformers, or was he just not troubled by Lisle's constant queries?

This is the first time that Cromwell refers to Calais having an infection of certain persons denying the Holy Sacrament of Christ's blessed body and blood, of such opinion as commonly they call 'Sacramentaries'. Cromwell's advice was to examine such people, and if found guilty to punish them taking care that 'no such errors pernicious be spread abroad there but utterly suppressed, banished and extincted'.[15]

We met Edward Clifford briefly back 1535. A kinsman of Sir Henry Knyvet, he was eventually given a room in the retinue when Henry Tourney's room became vacant. In August, Husee wrote that he was in trouble and likely to suffer for treason for counterfeiting the king's sign or seal. St Clare Byrne points out that due to the delay in gaining a room he may have turned to a life of crime forging documents to earn a living, but he could not have done it alone. As his correspondence shows, his handwriting and spelling is atrocious so someone else must have been actually producing the documents which included export licences for goods such as beer, cloth and horses. He was found guilty, to be drawn from Newgate to Tyburn, hanged, quartered and his head placed on London Bridge.

At the end of August Lisle finally got his permission to travel to England and meet the king at Dover. Honor originally travelled with him but returned early, quite possibly to care for her daughter Mary Basset who had been ill for several weeks. It must have been a relief for Lisle to be able to broach his concerns with his nephew and explain to him in person about the recent goings-on in Calais, especially touching on religious issues. Henry, pleased to see his uncle and hear what he had to say, invited Lisle to travel on with him to Canterbury.

He was back in Calais before the destruction of St Thomas Becket's shrine which caused outrage across the Christian world. This was not the only shrine to be destroyed in 1538; alongside the dissolution of the monasteries, shrines, images and idols were also demolished. The desecration of such a sacred site was thought a heinous act and condemned by the Pope. Thomas Becket, Archbishop of Canterbury, was murdered in 1170 after King Henry II is supposed to have said: 'Will no one rid me of this turbulent priest?' and four knights had taken it upon themselves to kill him. He was canonised in 1173 and since then hundreds of thousands of people made pilgrimage to his shrine each year leaving gifts of jewels and gold. Henry VIII, not satisfied with just the demolition of his shrine, is thought to have ordered his name be struck out of history's records and his bones be removed, burnt and his ashes scattered – or that's what the Pope declared. It is not actually known what happened to them and one theory suggests that the monks in the cathedral actually removed them and replaced them with that of the Abbott of Evesham.

Later, Thomas Derby, Clerk of the Privy Council, would write that 'it was arrested [attested] that his shrines and bones shuld be taken away and bestowed in suche place as the same shuld cause no superstition afterwards [as it is indeed among others of that sorte conveyed and buryed in a noble tower.'[16] While many people reeled in horror at the destruction of all they had held dear, they could do nothing about it. It was a confusing and worrying time.

Lisle may well have been horrified but he, like most of the population, had to be resigned to whatever the king decreed. Earlier in the year Cromwell had asked him to explain 'the dissension among you upon certain lewd words and the pulling down of the image of Our Lady in the Wall'. He went on to say:

as concerning the pulling down of the Image, though it be thought that many abuses and fond superstitions were maintained by the same, yet if it were taken down after any such sort as implied a contempt of common authority or might have made any tumult in the people, upon your signification thereof such like order shall be taken therein as shall be thought expedient.[17]

Lisle replied 'We esteem the offence as it shall please the King and your lordship to take it, though we cannot determine that it should be a contempt'.[18] And once again he reminds Cromwell he had written to him before about the matter.

And as touching a tumult, blessed be Our Lord, none such hath been, though I specially advertised your lordship of such things as were contained in my letters … which I did specially to the intent I might have knowledge from your lordship of the King's high pleasure, whereby the tumult might be eschewed, for I esteem that nothing more pernicious may be suffered in this his Highness' town.[19]

A set of injunctions would be issued to the clergy this year that underlined that the 'offering of money, candles or taper to images or relics, or kissing or licking the same'[20] should be discouraged and those images or relics so 'abused' should be taken down.

Lisle was probably none the clearer of how he was to deal with religious infractions. A more personal matter that was also bothering him was his lack of money and however exasperated he was with the Lord Privy Seal and his general lack of direction, he asked him to help. Cromwell was no pushover and he wasn't just going to give Lisle a handout. Instead he wanted Lisle's life-interest in Painswick. Lisle had asked for £100 to which Cromwell's response was that if he got what he wanted he would have 'many hundred pounds of him'.[21] Husee of course was involved in the negotiations and had to point out that Painswick was part of Honor's jointure. It made no difference to the Lord Privy Seal, who would wait for their answer knowing that really he gave them no choice.

When Lisle met with the king at Dover he had come away with the impression he would now receive a £400 annuity – a £200 raise on what he was currently receiving – and be granted the White Friars house in Calais, a suppressed property. Cromwell was of course responsible for the paperwork and until the decision over Painswick had been made there was no rush to sort any of it out. Lisle seems also to have misunderstood the king. It appears that a raise was agreed but not the exact amount, and it was down to Cromwell to arrange the particulars.

Husee, as always, would be his go-between, but in September he heard a horrible rumour that his master was dead. He waited anxiously for confirmation or a letter from Lisle to prove otherwise and in the meantime tried to find out which of Lisle's 'back friends' was spreading the 'bruit'. He wrote to Lisle to tell him, hoping it was not true and that he was 'waiting hourly for news'.[22] He must have felt a huge sense of relief when it came. By October Lisle was again depressed at the lack of attention to his suits and his desperation for money. He told Husee that God and the world had forsaken him. Husee was fast becoming not only Lisle's most efficient agent but his personal counsellor. He tried to reassure him:

What will there be said when your lordship, being ever called the pleasantest-witted in the world, should so suddenly be changed?

There is no doubt but your affairs shall prosper, and things shall frame as well as you can desire it. Therefore, in the honour of God, it shall please your lordship to extirpate these sudden desperate sorrows and fantasies out of the bottom of your stomach, and remit all to God, and he will unfeignedly redress all things at his pleasure. And therefore all these carnal and worldly things must be taken as they are, and all things to be used according unto the times that doth and shall rise which shall be healthful both for the body and soul. I have no doubt but your lordship will pardon [my] rude writing and accept the meaning, as of him [wh]ich desireth the preservation of your health and ho[no]r no less than his own heart blood.[23]

As Painswick was Honor's to dispose of she travelled over to England in November. She had other family matters to discuss with Cromwell and there was also the matter of Lisle's annuity that had not yet been approved, but it was not a good time to be at court. A conspiracy had supposedly been uncovered and it involved Lisle's kinsfolk.

While the situation was unfolding in London, Honor conducted her business – not a little disappointed when it became apparent that Lisle had promised Painswick to Cromwell and not only that, he had assured him of Honor's good will. She told Lisle 'What may I now do herein, your promise everyway considered?' She obviously felt she had been hemmed into a corner. Cromwell delayed their meeting but Honor was being well cared for. She had lodgings at court, attended a banquet 'partly made for me',[24] and met with the king. She told her husband that his nephew had asked after him and wished he had been there. Henry was just being pleasant – Lisle could have been there if he had been given licence.

When Honor finally met with Cromwell, they discussed several matters but he did not broach the subject of Painswick. Honor took matters into her own hands and in a very shrewd move asked that his interest in her lands was for his own self and no other. Back in 1534, Kingston had almost fallen out with Lisle over wood being felled on the estate and it was well known that he coveted Painswick and would gladly take ownership of it. Cromwell swore 'it should be for no creature but himself',[25] but he did indeed have plans to sell it to Sir William Kingston who would buy the property in May 1540. Lisle told his wife that in the matter of Painswick he remitted to her discretion and wisdom, but still he asked that she made 'true of my promise' to the Lord Privy Seal. She would write to him later in the year that she had indeed surrendered her right to Painswick and she forgave her 'own sweet heart root' although she recognised these were dangerous times and ended one particular letter with 'keep my letters secret, or burn them'.[26] And the king's pleasantries also came as Lisle's Pole and Courtenay relations were interrogated.

The Exeter conspiracy was a suspected plot by the Pole and Courtenay families to overthrow the king and place the 1st Marquess of Exeter on the throne. Castillon, the French ambassador, had reported:

The king told me a long time ago he wants to exterminate the House of Montagu that belongs to the White Rose, the Pole family, of which the Cardinal is a member. So far I don't know what he means to do about the Marquess [of Exeter, Henry Courtenay]. It looks as if he is searching for any excuse he can find to destroy them.[27]

As we have seen, assassins were sent after Reginald Pole, Lisle's cousin, but they had been unsuccessful. Now Henry would seek to destroy those that were in reach.

The Exeter conspiracy started in the summer of 1538 when Gervase Tyndall informed Cromwell of some information he had gleaned concerning the Countess of Salisbury's household. Tyndall had been staying at the house of Richard Ayer, a surgeon, close to one of Margaret's homes at Warblington, ostensibly for a cure for his ill health but more probably sent by Cromwell to find out all he could. Ayer had a loose tongue and much to say on the state of the Countess' household, but the most incriminating piece of evidence he had to share was that Henry Holland, a servant of Geoffrey Pole's, was taking messages to his brother Reginald by which 'all the secrets of the realm of England is known to the bishop of Rome'.[28]

Geoffrey Pole was arrested on 29 August and interrogated on 26 October. Under interrogation he implicated the marquess and marchioness of Exeter and his own brother Henry Pole, Lord Montagu, among others as wanting 'a change in this world without meaning any hurt to the king'.[29] This was treasonous talk and hinted of a plot and his interrogators wanted to know more. He was threatened with torture and not long after this first interrogation Geoffrey tried to kill himself. Husee reported to Lisle that Geoffrey was 'so in despair that he would have murdered himself and, as it was told me, hurt himself sore'.[30]

Another man, Jerome Ragland, also gave evidence against Lord Montagu, telling them Henry had spoken ill of the king, that he was 'full of flesh and unwieldy, and that he could not long continue with his sore leg'.[31] Geoffrey was interrogated again on 2 and 3 November 1538. The next day Henry Pole, Lord Montagu, and Henry Courtenay, Marquess of Exeter, were arrested.

Henry Courtenay, 1st Marquess of Exeter, was the king's cousin and kin to Lisle. His mother was Princess Catherine of York, the sixth daughter of King Edward IV. He had been a Gentleman of the Privy Chamber, a member of the Privy Council and one of Henry's closest companions. It was well known that Courtenay's religious beliefs, and especially his wife's, were of a Catholic nature although he was loyal to his king, supporting his divorce with Queen Katherine. Geoffrey Pole was the only one to implicate him in anything treasonous, claiming Exeter had said 'knaves rule about the king. I trust to give them a buffet one day.'[32] He also suggested that Exeter supported Reginald Pole and was passing on state secrets to Lord Montagu. It was all just rumour and snippets of conversations never meant to be heard outside of their circle.

Geoffrey was questioned again and again over the coming days and the more he said, the more he implicated his brother. He didn't like the king he said, and was disgusted at how he had handled the Pilgrimage of Grace. He echoed Ragland's story of the king's sore leg, saying his brother had said it would kill him and 'then we shall have jolly stirring'.[33] Montagu was purported to have said things like: 'The king is not dead, but he will die one day suddenly', and 'I like well the doings of my brother the Cardinal'.[34] But again this was all just talk. True it was now treason to utter anything against the king, but there was no actual evidence of a plot, rebellion, or any action taken to rob the king of his throne. When Montagu was questioned he answered with a resigned air and did his best to alleviate any suspicion against him, but he knew where this would all end.

And although she had not been implicated in any wrong-doing, Margaret, Countess of Salisbury, was questioned on 12 November 1538 by Sir William Fitzwilliam, Earl of Southampton, and Thomas Goodrich, Bishop of Ely, and three days later she was taken to Cowdray Castle,

Sir William Fitzwilliam's home, under house arrest. Her interrogators reported:

> Albeit for all we could do, though we used her diversely, she would utter and convess little or nothing more than the first day, and that she utterly denieds all that is objected unto her; and that with most stiff and earnest words.[35]

And Fitzwilliam is reported to have said:

> We have dealt with such a one, as men have not dealt withal before us; we may call her rather a strong and constant man, than a woman. For in all behaviour howsoever we have used her, she has showed herself so earnest, vehement, and precise, that more could not be.[36]

Lisle knew of the arrests of his kinsmen and would later write to Cromwell concerning the land the Marquess of Exeter had purchased from his stepson John Dudley. In the morbid way of land-grabbing from condemned men, he wanted to put his claim forward, 'if it be as is reported of the said Marquess of Exeter'.[37] He had also asked Husee to find any correspondence between himself and the marquess – land covenants relating to the above – but it may have also been a careful move as well. Husee could not find anything in England and so advised Lisle to look at home and in Honor's papers.

On 3 December Thomas Warley informed Lisle that the Marquess of Exeter was at Westminster for his trial. 'It is a heavy case that they should be false to the King, which is so gracious to his loving and true subjects. God send them what they deserve.'[38] Whether they did in fact deserve their fate is highly debatable, but on 9 December 1538 Henry Pole, Lord Montagu, Henry Courtenay, 1st Marquess of Exeter and Sir Edward Neville, Henry Pole's brother-in-law, who was reported to have said 'his highness was a beast and worse than a beast',[39] were beheaded at the Tower of London.

But the destruction of the Pole family was not yet done. Geoffrey would be pardoned early the following year. As Chapuys caustically commented: 'I am told his life is granted to him, but he must remain in perpetual prison; also ... he tried to suffocate himself with a cushion.'[40]

His mother's fate, however, was yet to come. Lisle could have done nothing to help them – no one could. Once Henry's mind was made up there was no reprieve. The Exeter conspiracy was a farce and when Lisle was in trouble himself he must have thought back to this time.

Someone that still needed Lisle's help was our old mariner John Cheriton. He had apparently written many letters that went unanswered and as usual he was in dire straits. The Count of Tando had taken his ship, its ordnance and freight. He wrote plaintively 'My lord I am undone for ever more, for they have imprisoned me so oft and taken from me all that I ever had without justice, and if that your lordship have not compassion on me I am as one undone for ever.'[41] The Count of Tando was actually Claude de Savoie, Captain of Marseilles. We don't know if Lisle replied directly to Cheriton but he did approach Anne de Montmorency, the Constable of France, giving a slightly different story. Yes, Cheriton's ordnance had been taken but it was because his ship had been wrecked along the coast of Marseilles. Lisle asked that the thirteen pieces of ordnance were returned. This is the last we hear of Cheriton in the *Lisle Letters* so perhaps the problem was solved or given his luck over the past years, he was probably still sailing the high seas.

He did however petition the king between 1540 and 1542 to be allowed to collect alms for his crew members that were enslaved at the same time he was captured by the Turks. He informed Sir John Russell, Lord Admiral at the time, that thirty-six of his men had been killed but that forty-six were still in captivity. He also mentioned he could be of use if given an official position as he knew inside information about Turkish galleys and fortifications. We don't know the results of his appeal but he appears eventually to have returned to his native Devon for the remainder of his life.

Sir William Fitzwilliam had been elevated to the peerage in 1537 as the 1st Earl of Southampton. Despite all the protestations and statutes now relating to the giving of rooms he wrote to Lisle to admit one Simon Lychlad to a gunner's room. He admitted he had no authority to grant the room himself and left it to Lisle's discretion. The room had become vacant after the death of Hugh Lychlad, so Simon was probably a relative. Lisle had one Walter Jonys in mind for the position and had been pushed to ask for his room by George Browne, Master of the Ordnance, who had asked him to write letters to his kinsman Sir Anthony Browne, who was also Sir William Fitzwilliam's half-brother. He thought perhaps he could grant two rooms to both of the men but Fitzwilliam, now taking the higher ground, advised Lisle not to go against the statutes. Lisle's weariness with the whole long-running situation of rooms comes in his comment that 'every officer here is master of his own room saving I, which doth not a little decay me in shortening of my life' (to be so used – was deleted after).[42]

And George Browne was causing problems of his own. Lisle informed Cromwell he was meddling with 'great distillations',[43] meaning alchemy. He wasn't sure how far he had gone and was loath to interrogate him due to his relationship with Sir Anthony Browne, so once again he was asking Cromwell for his advice.

It was with no small relief that Lisle's annuity was granted at the end of the year. Honor was home and they would share Calais' Christmas festivities together, hopeful for what the future might bring. Little did they know that time was beginning to run out.

Chapter Nine

Suspected Sacramentaries
1539

It wasn't long before Lisle's joy at receiving his annuity became a thing of the past. One of the first letters he received in the New Year was from Sir Brian Tuke, the king's treasurer, reminding him of his unpaid debts. Tuke asked him to send the money without delay, or if he was going to seek help from the king or Cromwell to do so immediately as he was now 'at the point of outlawry' for his debt. Tuke had tried to postpone any action against him time and time again, but this was serious now. He wrote:

> And my lord, if anybody show you that ye cannot be outlawed because ye be a Lord of the Parliament, or in the King's service of war and beyond the sea, Believe him not: for if extremity had been used against you, your lordship had been at outlawry vij years past and much more, but I had commandment to forbear you for a season, but not so long. This your lordship may be sure, that what I may do, playing the part of an honest man, I have done, and will do: but your lordship is so great a wise man that you know where my principal honesty resteth.[1]

It was a worry but given his debts had been long accruing Lisle did not seem eager to pay them off, even if he could.

Lisle was still anxious to do his duty and keep in favour with the king. Perhaps then more grants would come his way. He had heard of a pirate ship – a newly built galleon that had been prepared for war – that instead had been commandeered by 'sea robbers', and thought it might cause problems in the Channel. He informed the Captain of Dieppe and Seneschal of Boulogne to watch out for them.

England was on high alert against the possibility of invasion after a ten-year peace treaty was signed by Francis I of France and Charles V, the Holy Roman Emperor, the previous year. Not only that, but the Pope had finally made public the bull that excommunicated Henry and was urging the rulers of France, Spain and Scotland to rise against him.

Husee wrote that there was 'great preparation of armour and weapons, with all manner of warlike munitions'.[2] Troops were being mustered and defences built. Most famously Henry began the building of his coastal defences and thirty device forts along the south coast of England funded from the proceeds of the dissolution of the monasteries, a hugely expensive project costing £376,000 at the time.

Calais too was on alert. All members of the retinue were recalled, as were absent officers like Lord Sandys. Lisle was eager for news he could pass on. He regularly sent details he had gleaned on to Cromwell, as when he heard French troops were making their way into the Pale with a view to making new fortifications at Ardres, but when he sent out archers on horseback there was no sign of them. Still he thought they might yet come and he promised 'that good watch be kept abroad, as I shall not fail, God willing, to put the same in ure, secretly and without any bruit to be made, and have sure spyall upon the same'.[3]

But it seems that all his news was not welcome and when Husee wrote to Lisle in February, he told him that Cromwell had reacted badly to a recent letter he had sent. Cromwell said:

It was time for your lordship now to wax grave, and not to give credit to every light flying tale or sudden feigned news, but to certify things worthe penning, and not to be earnest not hasty in writing, without the thing be first very circumspectly foreseen and weighed, that the same may something likely appear or resemble to the truth when it shall be opened here, saying further that he knoweth how things frame there well enough.[4]

Perhaps Lisle was being too eager to share Calais news but he was in a difficult position. If something happened and he had not informed the Lord Privy Seal he would have to answer for it, so he continued to write whether Cromwell was interested or not. Husee also sent Lisle a gentle reminder to make sure his letters were properly sealed as he had received one which was open. Although the letter was not important if it had have been, his message could easily have been read.

In March Edward Seymour, now Earl of Hertford, was sent to inspect the fortifications at Calais and Guisnes underlining that the repairs to the defences and the victualling of the towns were now of high importance. After years of wrangling with Lisle and Honor over property and lands this visit had the unexpected side effect of rebuilding the relationship between the Seymours and the Lisles. Honor especially had set out to make him their ally and not their enemy, to the point that Seymour even told Husee that if ever Lisle needed help with his affairs, he would do his best to provide assistance.

As preparations for war built apace but with no hostilities actually breaking out, for Lisle the duties of being Lord Deputy rolled on much the same. There were the usual issues with rooms – regardless of the statutes they never went away and complaints from disgruntled members of the retinue or unhappy citizens of Calais. But now an issue that would trump them all that had been brewing for some time began to make waves.

Cromwell wrote in May that he had been informed 'that the town of Calais should be in some misorder by certain Sacramentaries alleged to be in the same', and that he marvelled that:

Your lordship, having good knowledge and experience of my good will and continual desire to the repression of errors and to the establishment of one perfect unity in opinion amongst us all, the King's Majesty's people and subjects, would not vouchsafe to give me some knowledge if there be any such lewd persons amongst you. I doubt not but that your lordship knoweth both how much I do esteem that the King's Highness' town as my duty requireth, and how well I have (I thank God) hitherto considered what danger might ensue unto it by diversity of opinion, specially in matters so high and weighty, doing ever mine office as I might to quiet all things with an honesty charity that have lightly insurged among you. But leaving this part I shall address myself to this purpose, which is to signify unto you that the King's Majesty, being desirous to know the truth of these matters, hath willed and commanded me to write unto you and to the rest of his Council there that you shall assemble yourselves together and make due and circumspect inquisition of this and all other such matters as do or may in anywise interrupt the quiet and unity that should be there amongst you.[5]

It is strange that Cromwell sent such a message to Lisle when Lisle continually wrote and told him what was going on in Calais, but Cromwell had heard rumours from the Earl of Hertford about the situation there and he might have felt his control over religious reform slipping as well as his influence with the king. It also smacks of protestation – that he had been doing all he could for Calais which, given the continual problems of victualling, the unanswered letters and the warnings not to over bother him – was not exactly true.

In May Lisle threatened to travel to England without licence once again. Tired of Calais and of being so far from the court, he could not speak for himself on any matter and he knew that there was some animosity towards him. But Husee told him he could not just leave charge of Calais and decide to travel on the promise of a licence as he said: 'I had leyther lose ij of my fingers than it should so chance.'[6] Lisle was frustrated but we get a sense that he often told Husee what he wanted to do, perhaps to urge him to sort out his affairs, with no real intention of taking such a chance. Certainly by now, he did not expect his nephew the king to support him if he transgressed.

His debts needed sorting out but he still had no money to pay them. Sir Brian Tuke wrote again reiterating what he had said in his January letter. He had put off Lisle's debts for so long – ten years or more – and he could no longer keep silent nor did he want to offend Lisle 'by process' against him. Interesting to note that Honor had taken to sending Tuke gifts such as baked partridges and carp, but still Lisle could not do anything to pay his dues. And there was an extra mouth to feed at home, as his daughter Frances had given birth to his first grandchild named Honor, after her grandmother. We don't know if it pleased him or not, but Husee commented on the fact that it was a girl and hoped that 'by God's grace at the next shot she shall hit the mark'.[7] A typical Tudor reaction to the birth of a daughter!

While he fretted about going to England to sort out his affairs, his cousin Margaret Pole, the Countess of Salisbury, at the age of 65 was attainted without trial. Her attainder read:

And where also Margaret Pole, Countess of Salisbury, and Hugh Vaughan, late of Beckener, in the County of Monmouth, yeoman, by instigation of the devil, putting apart the dread of Almighty God, their duty of allegiance, and the excellent benefit received of his Highness, have not only traitorously confederated themselves with the false and abominable traitors Henry Pole, Lord Montagu, and Reginald Pole, sons to the said countess, knowing them to be false traitors, but also have maliciously aided, abetted, maintianed, and comforted them in their said false and abominable treason, to the most fearful peril of his Highness, the commonwealth of this realm, &c., the said marchioness and the said countess be declared attained, and shall suffer the pains and penalties of high treason.[8]

Margaret would be sent to the Tower in November where she would stay for the next two years. Sir William Fitzwilliam had become exasperated by her during her stay under house arrest at his home and had written to Cromwell: 'I beg you to rid me of her company, for she is both chargeable and troubleth my mind.'[9] It appears that his wife was troubled by having the countess in her home and Fitzwilliam had had to take her with him at times, 'for in nowise would she tarry behind me, the said lady being in my house'.[10]

If there was ever a warning to Lisle not to overstep the mark, it was now. It was a letter to Lisle from John Worth that tells us of the physical evidence – although probably fabricated – for the Countess' fall.

There was a coat-armour found in the Duchess [sic] of Salisbury's coffer, and by the one side of the coat there was the King's Grace his arms of England, that is the lions without the flowers de lys, and about the whole arms was made pansies for Poles and marigolds for my Lady Mary ... And betwixt the marigold and the pansy was made a tree to rise in the midst, and on the tree a coat of purple hanging on a bough in token of the coat of Christ, and on the other side of the coat all the Passion of Christ. Pole intended to have married my Lady Mary and betwixt them both should again arise the old doctrine of Christ.[11]

Henry could not get to Reginald Pole and he was anxious the Cardinal had too much influence in Europe. With the backing of Rome, the king feared Pole would arrive in England at the head of a papal army, marry his daughter Mary and take the crown. Both Margaret and the executed marquess of Exeter held vast amounts of land in the south of England and along the coast. If they were sympathetic to an invasion, their land could be a starting point and Henry wanted it under his control. Pole was still a threat to the crown, or so the king thought, and if he could not get to him, his family was the next best thing. It was no surprise then that Henry was not considering Lisle's request to travel to England.

Sir Nicholas Carew was one of the men who had been executed in March for his supposed part in the Exeter conspiracy. His position of Captain of Rysbank in the Pale was now given to his kinsman Sir George Carew. This Carew was no friend to Lisle and had been nominated for the post by Cromwell. He would write regular reports to the Lord Privy Seal about the state of Rysbank and he was not adverse to mentioning the Lord Deputy. In one letter written in May he told Cromwell that Lisle had given an order that the Bible should not be read at mass and service time.

April 1539 year saw the publication of the first authorised Bible in English that had been prepared by Myles Coverdale, on the orders of Cromwell. Priests were instructed to provide 'one book of the bible of the largest volume in English, and the same set up in some convenient place within the said church that ye have care of, whereas your parishioners may most commodiously resort to the same and read it'.[12]

Carew's own leanings towards reform are shown by his comment that 'the grief is not a little to those that favour God's word to have any time forbid them from the reading thereon',[13] and the fact that he made such a comment to Cromwell shows he knew he would find a sympathetic ear. Lisle, however, was acting in accordance with the King's Proclamation for Uniformity in Religion, a precursor to the Act of Six Articles that was issued in April. It stated that no one should read the Bible 'with any loud or high voices, and specially during the time of divine service'.[14] It was difficult to keep up with the constant changes to religious doctrine but Lisle was trying his best to go along with the king's orders.

Religious change was unrelenting. There was another Act of Suppression in May 1539 which covered the larger monastic sites. Nobles who paid for properties could then fund the building of their own homes, like Wriothesley did, by stripping the properties of furniture, wall hangings and other goods and selling on these and building materials like glass, stone and lead. But it wasn't just the nobility who gained from the dissolution of the monasteries. Local people also looted the vacant properties. One of Cromwell's agent said:

> The poor people thoroughly in every place be so greedy upon these houses when they be suppressed that by night and day, not only of the towns, but also of the country, they do continually resort as long as any door, window iron or glass or loose lead remaineth in any of them.[15]

But they lost out in other ways when the monasteries closed. They had provided charity, health care and education in local areas and the nobility that took over as landowners provided little to make up for what communities had lost. Monasteries had also employed local people as servants, cooks, gardeners and cleaners, as well as providing respite for travellers with accommodation and refreshment.

Those that lived in the monasteries – monks, canons, friars and nuns – found themselves homeless. Some had hidden relics or jewels from the visiting commissioners and fled into exile. Others were pensioned off and the less fortunate who failed to comply with the king's wishes were executed. Henry VIII also gained from dispersing the members of religious orders – now there were fewer people to question his supremacy and the nobles that had profited had every reason to support their king all the more. The last monastery to be dissolved was Waltham Abbey in March 1540. The disbandment, stripping and destruction of some of England's most beautiful buildings is thought to have swelled Henry's coffers by over a million pounds.

Following Cromwell's letter in May about the sacramentaries in Calais, Husee had been questioned by the Earl of Hertford as to 'what business there was ado concerning the Sacrament'. Husee denied any knowledge but Hertford pressed further, telling him that he knew the Council of Calais was of two parts, working in contrary ways. Cromwell had also asked Hertford of his opinion. Husee reliably informed Hertford that the Council were to be trusted but he warned Lisle there were others saying differently and that 'such things as are certified are not truth but surmised, and maliciously imagined and invented'.[16]

In fact the Council was divided between those that held reformist views and others who were more conservative, but despite this disparity they were doing their duty and investigating those in Calais who were believed to be sacramentaries, and others causing religious tensions. They had written to Cromwell several times and sent him the depositions of such people but as Lisle put it, he was 'long sore to have answer of'.[17] Cromwell was prevaricating again, but in May he did send one of his lengthiest letters to Lisle, although for all its length, it said very little.

Cromwell, possibly in a bid to protect the reformers of Calais – while playing for time in the hope the king would push forward with religious reform – gave Lisle and the Council no strict instructions, answered in vague terms and evaded any definite statement. As St Clare Byrne points out, Lisle was damned if he did and damned if he didn't. If he does not inform the Lord Privy Seal of what is happening in Calais he is not doing his duty, and if he does inform him he gets no answers.

Cromwell said:

> it is sore to note any man for a sacramentary unless he that shall be the author of the infamy know well what a sacramentary is. And yet is it more sore to note a commune officer put in place to advise and reform others of so heinous a crime, except it might be duly and evidently proved against him. I mean this by the Commissary, the depositions against whom be not most weighty and substantial.[18]

He was basically saying to be sure of the facts before blaming anyone, especially concerning Sir John Butler, commissary of Calais, described by some as a zealous reformer. Butler was Cranmer's official representative and there had been many complaints against him ranging from his keeping of a mistress to theft and murder, but it was with religion that the Calais council were concerned.

Butler himself had complained about Lisle and others in 1535 saying:

> At divers times heretofore I have openly declared unto my Lord Deputy, the mayor, and all other of the King's Council here, the oath of renouncing the Bishop of Rome's pretenced power, which

was stablished in the last parliament ... but such oath is there none taken, used, or spoken of among them, whereof much papistry doth reign still, and chiefly among them that be Rulers.[19]

Lisle must have heard he was being slandered because he wrote to Cranmer that he was being accused of being a papist, but at the time Cranmer assured him that his commissary had never spoken an evil word against him. Their relationship had obviously not improved over time and now, four years later, the situation was coming to a head.

Lisle told Cromwell that he wasn't a malicious person and was doing his duty as Lord Deputy, but he now knew that Cromwell was no help. The Council informed Archbishop Cranmer of Butler's misconduct – there were a number of charges against him including that he 'did say and affirm that a draught of Aqua Vitae bought at John Spicer's of Calais, grocer, and drunken up, should do a man as much good as the body of Christ contained in the blessed Sacrament of the altar could do'.[20] They felt that it was time for a new commissary 'whereby we think the people which been now in much division, discord and variety of opinion, may be brought into unity, quietness and accord'.[21]

In a wise move, Lisle wrote to Sir Anthony Browne of 'the erroneous opinions against the Sacrament' at Calais and the 'other evil opinions concerning the Scripture and in banding of certain persons for maintenance of the same, wherewith I have been continually vexed and trouble this ij years'.[22] He also mentioned another set of Calais citizens that caused trouble – the vinteners and the constables – who were influenced by persons 'being of the said opinions and evil sort', and closed his letter by asking Browne to keep his message close for if Cromwell was to find out about it, 'I were half undone'.[23] It is clear that religious dissension in Calais was reaching boiling point.

By now it was not just the Council but others that had been made aware of the situation in Calais, such as the Earl of Hertford and Sir Anthony Browne, so Cromwell could not continue to ignore the fact that these reformers were going unpunished – something that may have added to charges of heresy later being levelled against him.

Thomas Boyes, one of the burgesses now representing Calais at parliament, was in London and had been asked to put down in writing the situation in the town. He was obviously loyal to Lisle as he told him that his 'book' would only do him and the Council 'good and no hurt', but what was more worrying was that he told the Lord Deputy he had many enemies at court.

> I heard one say unto Thomas Broke that you were a Pharisee, and I made him answer that he was a false knave and an heretic that so said; and further I said unto him, Because your lordship rebuketh seditious and erroneous persons therefore in no wise they can abide you.[24]

Boyes duly wrote his book 'concerning the misbehaviour and the disobedience of a great number of persons in Calais', and had delivered it to the king by 21 June when he wrote again telling Lisle: 'I will be a Right Champion in this matter'.[25] He also reported that due to the act and new provisions to ensure uniformity, it was expected more dissenters would be arriving from Calais and Lisle should send over any evidence against them. This Lisle duly did and there were witnesses as well, but it seems that delay tactics were being used. The Council informed the bishops of Bath, Chichester and Norwich of the facts surrounding Butler's disgrace, but Husee informed his master that 'little was being laid to the Commissary's charge'.[26] He didn't know whether Cromwell had received the depositions but thought it wise to send copies to the bishops.

Cromwell's press for reform was not progressing as swiftly as he would have liked, the king would always remain essentially conservative in his views, as were others of his council. In May, parliament had met and agreed that a committee should determine religious doctrine and decide on certain points that the Ten Articles had not made clear. The Ten Articles had been agreed in July 1536 'to establish Christian quietness and unity', but had led to more questions than answers, especially:

> whether the Eucharist could be the true body of Christ without transubstantiation,
>
> whether it needed to be given to the laity under both kinds,
>
> whether vows of chastity needed to be observed as part of divine law,
>
> whether clerical celibacy should be compulsory,

whether private masses were required by divine law,

whether auricular confession (that is, confession to a priest) was necessary as part of divine law.[27]

Their decisions on each point formed the Act of Six Articles which became enshrined in law in June 1539 and Cromwell could no longer ignore Lisle, the Council and their complaints., There was some leeway however, as transgressions occurring before 26 February could be pardoned as per the Proclamation for Rites and Ceremonies of the Church. Yet by the beginning of July, most of the Calais dissenters had been investigated and witnesses examined and Cranmer agreed that a 'discreet priest' was needed as Calais' new commissary. He promised to try to find one, although he thought it would be no easy task as 'not many learned men wanted to travel beyond the sea and out of the realm'.[28]

Thomas Broke was an alderman, treasurer and Calais' other member of parliament and he had spoken out against the Act of Six Articles, although he was warned not to do so 'as he loved his life'.[29] Speaking out earnt him a place in Foxe's *Book of Martyrs*, where his speech can be read in more detail. Sir William Kingston was disgusted with the man and told him he would happily bring a faggot to help burn him if he was executed for heresy, earning him a reprimand from the speaker for interfering with the freedom of debate. Broke also intervened at the trial of Ralph Hare, a soldier of Calais and another accused of heresy, and would later find himself in the Fleet prison at the same time as John Butler, Calais' commissary. It seems that the king was entirely sick of the whole affair when he made a comment to one of the retinue at court: 'I have more ado with you Calais men than with all my realm after.'[30]

More information on what Foxe termed the 'persecution in Calais' of Protestant reformers can be found in his book. He lists those that were persecuted and those that were the persecutors. Lisle, he wrote, was 'of a most gentle nature, and of a right noble blood', so no blame for the situation was levelled at him. However, it was the evil Honor who 'fiercely set on, and incessantly enticed' her husband, and he continued by calling her 'an utter enemy to God's honour; and in idolatry, hypocrisy, and pride, incomparably evil, she being daily and hourly incited and provoked by Sir Thomas Palmer, knight, and John

Rookwood [Rokewood], esquire.'[31] Of course Foxe was writing from his own standpoint, but it shows just how divided feeling was and how much it was colouring the climate in Calais.

Lisle was stuck in the middle and the religious changes and what they meant for Calais would remain an issue over the next months. He continued to inform Cromwell of incidences he believed were contrary to the king's will – whether he wanted to hear it or not – and was starting to take a stronger tone with him.

In August he told the Lord Privy Seal:

I beseech you not to give credit to every light, seditious person that have or hereafter shall make unto your lordship suggestion against me or the King's Council here; for if your lordship shall give favourable ear unto the complaints and tales of light, obstinate and contentious persons ye shall not only encourage them to ensue the same and continually to disturb you with every light matter, but also cause them to set little by, vilipende and disobey me and the rest of the said Council here.[32]

Husee had warned Lisle: 'It may chance that all such friends as are now may decay, for men are mortal.'[33] He had sent over four rolls of recent proclamations for Lisle to peruse including those concerning beggars, fishing and hawks, hunting in the king's grounds and one concerning the sacrament of the altar and other religion matters. Following this he received news that the bishops of Salisbury and Worcester had resigned and a rumour that Bishop Latimer had been sent to the Tower for opposing the Six Articles. He would later be released but others were not so lucky. Husee wrote on 8 July that the vicar of Wandsworth, with another priest and two friars, was hanged, drawn and quartered.

Lisle finally received permission to travel to England at the end of August. He told Honor he had made it over safely without being sick and he was 'not a little proud' that he had become 'so strong a seaman'.[34] He was well received by the king and 'was never more made of, nor better entertained' in London and at Canterbury.[35] He was also happy with his conversations with Cromwell and had raised several issues including a breach of the ordinances. Nine men had been involved and it was agreed four of the retinue would be dismissed, as well as Henry Tourney who we have met before. It was a short-lived victory. On Lisle's return to Calais he made the offenders vacate their rooms and left them empty until he knew the king's pleasure, but just weeks later Cromwell denied he had ever given him leave to dismiss them. Husee relayed Cromwell's comment that he had agreed seditious men should be sent over to London, but hadn't said they should be dismissed from their livings and that many people there 'did speak ill of it'.[36] The men who claimed to have no idea why they had been dismissed had their own supporters at court, not least the Lord Privy Seal who was once more prevaricating and putting Lisle in an tenuous position.

The Calais situation for Lisle was in no way improving and as before, his mental health must have suffered for being caught between the king, Cromwell and the duties he had to undertake as Lord Deputy. His financial affairs were still in difficulties and would ever remain so. Elis Gruffudd, sometimes known as 'the soldier of Calais', was employed by Sir Robert Wingfield, the mayor of Calais and resident in the town between 1520 and 1524. After a spell in London looking after Wingfield's house he returned to Calais in 1529 and joined the garrison. He mentioned in his chronicle *Cronicl o Wech Oesoedd* (Chronicle of the Six Ages), which covers the history of the world from the beginning up to the year 1552, that Lisle lived off dead men's pay, referring to a payment that was made when a member of the retinue died and now Sir Brian Tuke was again reminding him of his debts. Tuke knew he had seen the king lately and thought perhaps something of this nature might have been discussed, but yet again he had heard nothing. Feeling that he could not tell whether 'all the favour and sparing that I have done hitherto concerning the same should do either your lordship or me good or harm',[37] he humbly implored Lisle to do something about his debt, but as far as we know Lisle left Tuke unanswered.

Lisle was now too busy with preparations for a very important guest. Back in October Cromwell wrote to Lisle to improve the town, especially the Exchequer House.

> The king's Majesty's pleasure is that you shall view his Grace's house here called the Exchequer, that with all diligence all things therein necessary to be amended may be undelayedly repaired... Furthermore, his Majesty would that you should cause the streets

and lanes there to be viewed for the pavements, and where any default is, to give commandment to those which should repair the same to see it immediately amended, endeavouring yourselves to put all other things within the said town in the most honest and cleanly order you can devise...[38]

Although the guest's identity wasn't mentioned by name, it was obvious that Calais was to host someone that the king wanted to impress. The town – not visited by royalty since Henry visited with Anne Boleyn in 1532 – was in need of much restoration. The walls needed repairing, the Lantern Gate renovating; everything needed a fresh coat of paint and the streets needed to be cleaned. Henry sent over a barrage of men to do the work and Lisle had to make sure that the king's orders were carried out. They included:

9 free masons, 4 sawyers, a carpenter's apprentice, 14 bricklayers out of England, 15 of the town and marches, 10 bricklayers' prentices, 18 labourers making mortar, 9 water bearers, 85 mortar bearers, 50 bearers of chalk to the bricklayers, 29 labourers digging in the foundation, &c., 30 boys bearing of brick and chalk, 15 labourers burning of lime and hewing of chalk at Bullen Well, 6 slakers of lime, 3 water-bearers to them, 4 labourers lading cartes at the brickery, 5 working in the Braies at 9¾d., 5 cutting turfs at 8d., 8 casting earth behind the turfs, 2 watchers, 8 daily labourers, 4 labourers appointed by the King's bill, and 4 clerks.[39]

The town needed to be made fit for a queen – Henry's fourth wife, Anne of Cleves, to be precise – as well as her entourage and the English nobles that were sent to greet her. Early in December, Anne reached Gravelines, just a few miles from Calais and was met by Lisle:

the lieutenant of the Castle, the Knight Porter, and the marshal of Calais, Sir George Carew, captain of Resbanke, and the captain of the Spears, well appointed with great horses, and with them the men of arms, in velvet coats and gold chains, and all the archers in the ing's livery well appointed.[40]

to officially escort her on towards Calais. Outside the town, she was welcomed by William Fitzwilliam, Earl of Southampton and Lord Admiral:

> who had in his companie thirtie gentlemen of the king's household, as Sir Francis Brian, Sir Thomas Seimer [Seymour], and others, beside a great number of gentlemen of his owne retinue clad in blue veluet, and crimson satin, and his yeomen in damaske of the same colours. The mariners of his ship were apparelled in satin of Bridges, cotes & slops of the same colour. The lord admerall brought her into Calis by lantern Gate.[41]

The king's ships the *Lyon* and the *Sweepstake* fired so much ammunition, 'a peale of ordnance shot off ... as was maruellous to the hearers',[42] that a great pall of smoke enveloped English and German nobles alike, not to mention the king's bride-to-be. Lady Lisle escorted Anne to the Exchequer to refresh herself. Henry's bride-to-be was supposed to stay for two day but instead it would be over two weeks until she could travel onwards to her new life in England.

Honor did her best to make sure Anne was comfortable and had everything she needed. Her own daughter, Anne Basset, had been selected for the queen's household in England and Lady Lisle wrote to give her news of the young lady that would soon become her mistress. Anne replied:

> I humbly thank your ladyship of the news you write me of her Grace, that she is so good and gentle to serve and please. It shall be no little rejoicement to us, her Grace's servants here, that shall attend daily upon her. And most comfort to the king's majesty, whose Highness is not a little desirous to have her Grace here.[43]

Anne may also have been providing the king some comfort as she was rumoured to be his mistress.

Henry was growing more and more impatient to meet the woman who would be his fourth queen – a woman he had never seen in the flesh but only in a portrait – but as the weather was not suitable for the sea voyage plans were made to entertain Anne in Calais. Fitzwilliam took precedence, taking her on a tour of the harbour to show her the king's fleet. There were banquets and Anne learnt a card game that Henry liked so that she would be able to play with her new husband, although Fitzwilliam was a little concerned it might not be proper.

Finally the weather changed and Anne departed Calais for her new home and new husband on 27 December. Lisle probably sighed with relief but for him, all the visit had really done was postpone the most terrible time in his life.

Chapter Ten

Commission and Conspiracy
1540–1542

It was clear to all that the king was not impressed with his fourth bride, Anne of Cleves. In a fit of petulant rage he had refused to marry her, but this was one time where he did not get his own way and to avert a diplomatic crisis they were married on 6 January 1540. Henry told his Lord Privy Seal: 'if it were not to satisfy the world and my realm, I would not do that I must do this day for none earthly thing'.[1] He was in a foul temper and clearly blamed Cromwell for his role in negotiating such a match.

For Lisle 1540 started as normal, but Henry's religious changes were settling in and were far more conservative than the reformers had hoped – Cromwell included. Lisle knew that the situation in Calais would take more than Cromwell to sort out – his letters went unanswered, replies, when he got them, were evasive, and when prisoners were sent to England Cromwell sought to have them released and returned to Calais.

The Duke of Norfolk was sent on a diplomatic mission to Francis I and stopped in Calais between 24 and 27 February. He was a friendly ear to Lisle who asked him to intervene and talk to the king about the state of Calais. Norfolk was happy to help but he had an ulterior motive – he saw it as a way to bring Cromwell down. There was a swelling anti-Cromwell faction at court – Norfolk, Gardiner and other conservative men – who felt the Lord Privy Seal had too much power and wanted too much religious reform and they sought ways to stop him.

When Norfolk returned to England he had an audience with the king and within two weeks commissioners were sent to Calais. During this time Lisle received his last extant letter from his most loyal and trustworthy servant, Husee. During the previous year his correspondence and the news he had to give had lessened. Neither of them knew that this would be their final correspondence and Husee gave his usual update on

Lisle's business, telling his master that in his next letter he hoped to send his lordship good news. He wrote on 3 March and on the 9th a royal commission to look into Calais' state of affairs was appointed.

Lisle was to be included in the investigation of Calais affairs – a sign of trust and the esteem his nephew held him in. Although they would look at Lisle's role as deputy and his administration, religious issues were paramount. It is suggested that Cromwell tried to stop the commissioners or delay them at least, afraid of what they might find. The king apparently had not told him of their departure. Henry too was becoming more suspicious of his secretary's motives, but there was nothing the Lord Privy Seal could do. He must have known that he was on shaky ground by now.

The commissioners including the Earl of Sussex, Lord St John, Sir John Gage and Sir John Baker arrived on Tuesday 16 March and would stay for the next six weeks, interrogating 'heretics, schismatics, and seditious persons'. The town was in turmoil. As Foxe put it: 'such fear and distrust assaulted all men, that neighbour distrusted neighbour, the master the servant, the servant the master, the husband the wife, the wife the husband, and almost every one the other'.[2] The commissioners found numerous cases to bring to the attention of the king and they sent their first report back on 5 April.

Adam Damplip, alias George Bucker, who back in 1538 had caused some consternation with his religious sermons, was thought to have been one of the main perpetrators of religious dissent in the town. Damplip, once chaplain to the Bishop of Rochester, had travelled across Europe after his master's execution and visited Cardinal Pole in Rome, returning via Calais he had been persuaded to stay by two members of the retinue, Thomas Lancaster and William Stevens. Stevens was questioned about his involvement with Damplip and charged with hiring him to preach 'false and erroneous doctrine, whereby the town, being divided and at contention with itself, might easily be overcome and won by the frenchmen'.[3] Stevens reply to the charges was that if he had done so it was because Lisle had asked him to, 'if it had been treason indeed, he must have been more faulty'.[4] And it was true. Lisle and Honor had welcomed this man to their home and at first were pleased with his sermons. 'Lisle swore he never heard a better collation or sermon',[5] and he was not the only one to be taken in by Damplip:

The Lord Deputy and a great part of the Council, gave him marvellous great praise and thanks for it; and the said Lord Deputy offered unto him a chamber in his own house, to dine and sup every meal at his own mess, to have a man or two of his to wait upon him, and to have whatsoever it were that he lacked.[6]

However, Damplip thanked him for his offer but asked that Lisle find him a 'quiet and honest place in the town'.[7] Williams Stevens was asked to give him lodging which he duly did, and meals were sent over from Lisle's kitchen. He also provided him with clothing and coin.

But it was not long before Lisle had informed Cromwell that a young priest coming from Germany had spoken about the sacrament in a way 'much varying' from the king's book. Lisle, as usual, had asked for Cromwell's advice but received no reply, 'for I have written your lordship iij letters concerning this same self matter and could never hear word of answer'.[8] As Damplip had continued to preach, his sermons had become more subversive.

Damplip either travelled to England by his own volition or was called to answer for the concerns around his sermons. He was interviewed by Cranmer who felt he was of 'right good knowledge and judgement',[9] and should be allowed to return to Calais and then sent on to Cromwell, but before he could be interrogated or questioned any further he disappeared.

He was again apprehended in 1539 and accused of preaching that the body and blood of Christ were not present in the sacrament. The chronicler, Elis Gruffudd, later wrote there were sixty witnesses who swore to Damplip's heresy. He was incarcerated in the Marshalsea prison and would later be released, but only to return to Calais to await execution. Instead of being charged with heresy he was charged with being a traitor for accepting money from Cardinal Pole and was executed in 1543. Lisle may well have been wary of providing more information on Damplip as he had so readily welcomed him to his home. The commissioners, however, did not find Lisle at fault, but agreed that Damplip had fomented heresy and divided the religious opinions of Calais citizens. But his story showed the possible connection between Lisle, a friend of Pole's, and the Cardinal himself, and it would add to the next affair that implicated the Lord Deputy.

What would become known as the Botolf conspiracy was unfolding while the commissioners were in Calais. During their investigation one Clement Philpot, Lisle's servant, was questioned and he told them of a plot to capture the town. The main instigator was Sir Gregory Botolf ('Gregory Sweet-Lips', so named by Gruffudd for his charming, smooth-tongued talk) who was Lisle's chaplain from 1538.

Botolf had been described as 'a man of good discretion and honest behaviour',[10] but also 'the most mischievous knave that was ever born'[11] by Sir Oliver Browne, another of Lisle's chaplains who was aware that he had stolen church plate from the chantry house of St Gregory in Canterbury. In January, Botolf, Philpot and one John Woller, were given leave to travel to England by Lisle. On 5 February the men waited outside Calais' walls to catch the night boat, but Botolf slipped away into the darkness and made for Rome where he supposedly met with the Pope and Cardinal Pole to hatch a plan to take Calais.

Both Clement Philpot and Edward Corbett were involved in his plans. Philpot was from a good Hampshire family and had been recommended to Lisle's service by Sir Anthony Windsor. Husee felt he was 'a proper young man' and suitable to marry Lisle's stepdaughter, Philippa. He too had joined the Lisle household in 1538 around the same time as Botolf and they became good friends, sharing a chamber. We don't know much about Edward Corbett but he was employed by Lisle in a secretarial capacity. Corbett's role was to get Lisle to sign a licence for Botolf to go to the University of Louvain, ostensibly to study but in reality to work on their plot. Corbett knew that Lisle easily signed papers without reading them – something that Husee had warned his master about previously.

Botolf returned to Calais while Philpot was still in England but he didn't stay long. In conspiratorial fashion, Botolf showed Corbett ten papal crowns that were to be melted down and made into three rings – one for each of them to show their bond and inscribed with their initial, 'a P for Philpot, a C for Corbett, and a B for Botolf!' Corbett told him he had asked Lisle for his licence which was under consideration and he had approached Honor to help speed things up, but in the meantime Botolf was going to wait at Bourbourg for Philpot to join him. From there he wrote to Corbett regarding some possessions he had left behind. Corbett then approached Lisle for a licence to go to Gravelines to meet Botolf and when Lisle asked him the reason he told him:

I shewed his Lordship that I had bought Sir Gregory's bed and chest that was in his chamber, and that I promised him to bring him his money at that day, and my Lord said, 'What doth he there so long?' And I said he tarried there for Philpot's coming home, because he knoweth not where is much of his apparel which he should have with him. And my Lord said, 'Might not the fool have tarried as well here as to spend his money there?'[12]

Lisle had no idea that anything untoward was happening and allowed Corbett licence to travel. Botolf wrote again to remind him of his own licence needed to travel to Louvain and it shows how gullible they thought Lisle was:

No doubt if ye make the writing ready to his hand he will not fault to sign and seal it. If he suspect anything then take my lady's advice, showing her ladyship in that I most heartily besought you to procure for me of my said lord and lady that same writing.[13]

On 26 March Botolf met with Philpot at Bourbourg to outline his plans to take Calais. Philpot was to take control of the Lantern Gate during the time when herring was bought and sold and the guard on the gate relaxed. Philpot was to work from within Calais' walls, overcoming the watch with some handpicked men, while Botolf attacked from outside. Philpot claimed Botolf told him:

That you, with a dozen persons well appointed for the same purpose, shall enter the watch and destroy them. That done, ye shall recule back with your company and keep the stairs. And at the same time when you begin I with my company shall be ready to scale the walls over the gate … when we are entered the leads, there is but a little door to be broke up, which shall soon be done, where then we may enter the town easily. I will have five or six hundred men that shall enter with me on the first brunt: the most part shall be gunners, their pieces shall shoot four shots: they shall be made for the purpose. And as many as will resist, shall be destroyed without mercy.[14]

Philpot was obviously not sure this would work, but when he questioned Botolf he was assured that 'they would have aid soon after both by sea and land'. Money would also be made available for Philpot to become Captain of Rysbank which would give him authority to man the gate. It is hard to gauge whether Philpot believed this could actually happen when he was no soldier, not even a member of the retinue and would in no way be accepted for the position.

Botolf's swaggering and bravado makes the whole plot questionable. Was he really being funded by the Pope? Where were the 500–600 soldiers or the aid from sea and land coming from and did they truly exist? There is some suggestion that Pope Paul III had given Botolf his support, but perhaps it was just a story. Philpot certainly believed him and swore Botolf had said:

> I shall get the town of Calais into the hands of the Pope and Cardinal Pole; this was the matter that I went to Rome for; and I have consulted with the Holy Father the Pope and with the reverend father Cardinal Pole, who is a good Catholic man as ever I reasoned with; and when I had declared everything of my mind unto them, no mo but we iij together in the Pope's chamber, where we reasoned upon many matters, I had not a little cheer of the Pope and Cardinal Pole and all the Cardinals, as the Pope himself did command me to have; and after this at all times I might enter the Pope's chamber at my pleasure and speak with him.[15]

After Botolf outlined his plans to Philpot he left for Ghent, accompanied by Corbett's servant John Browne. They were met on the road by Sir John Mason and 'Francis the Post' who were suspicious of the travellers. Browne explained:

> And Francis asked me what countryman I was, and I said, 'An Englishman', and where I dwelt, and I said, 'At Calais', and he said 'With who?' and I said 'With one of my Lord Deputy's gentlemen', and he did ask me my master's name, and I said 'Mr. Corbett'. Then called he aloud, 'Mr. Corbet! Ho!' [sic] And I said that my master was not there, and he asked, 'Who, then?' And I said that it was a gentleman of my Lord Deputy's house. 'What call you him?' And I

said I did not know his name, and he asked whither he held on, and I said, 'To Louvain, to the University.' Then he said, 'Belike he is some student?' 'Yea', said I, 'he is a priest, one of my lord's chaplains'; and then they rode apace away. And he [Botolf] heard us and then he was angry with me because that I said I was Mr. Corbet's servant, and I said that I will never deny my master so long as I knew him for a true man. And then he was angry with me, for me would a'had me say that I had been his man.[16]

Botolf gave Browne quite the run around, getting him to wait and fobbing him off to get rid of him, presumably so that he could meet with other conspirators, but he did want Browne to accompany him to the ambassador's house. There he had left some letters to be sent to Calais, but when he went to retrieve them he found they were gone. Sir Thomas Wyatt, then the English ambassador in Ghent, would eventually read them and forward them to England for the king's attention. Something in them had aroused his suspicions.

Philpot, meanwhile, had thought better of involving himself in such a treasonous plot. He approached the commissioners in Calais with the story that he had just found out what Botolf was planning. But he had left it too late to claim he was an informer rather than a conspirator and admitted he had known about it for eight days. He tried to make them believe that he had waited so long because he wanted to tell the king in person, but it was no good. He knew he was in serious trouble yet still he outlined all he knew to the commissioners.

Philpot was told to write a letter to Botolf in a bid to lure him back to Calais, but it didn't work. The main instigator of the plot had reached Louvain and remained there. The mayor of Louvain was informed that Botolf was a thief and had stolen church property in a bid to have him incarcerated. He was arrested but freed. Cardinal Pole interceded on his behalf and the last we hear of Botolf he was being entertained by the Bishop of Liege. Where he escaped to from there we don't know, and although attainted by an act of parliament, he was never brought to justice. Both Philpot and Corbett were sent to the Tower on 24 April. Corbett too seemed to have evaded punishment and it would be Philpot who would endure a traitor's death.

Henry sent for Lisle on 17 April to discuss matters. Much had happened and he wanted to talk to him personally. On the surface, there was nothing in the letter to cause alarm:

Right trusty and right well beloved cousin and councillor, whereas by our right entirely beloved cousin and councillor the Duke of Norfolk, as by your letters you have desired to repair hither, as well as for certain other causes, and specially concerning the order of that our town and marches to make declaration of the behaviour of such of our officers and subjects there, who as it appeareth have in such wise forgotten themselves and also their duties towards us as they seem to pay no regard towards you, being their as our principal minister, we be now therefore desirous to hear your advice therein and to consider and declare our mind and pleasure unto yourself in that behalf.[17]

He was required to leave the keys of the town with Robert Radcliffe, the 1st Earl of Sussex and Sir John Gage and make haste for London. Lisle was hoping that his recall would lead to a preferment or permanent recall and he set off knowing that he had been vindicated by the commissioners. He looked forward to being at court again and being able to talk to his nephew the king. All would be explained and all would be well.

He set off as soon as he could and was at Westminster Palace by Friday 23 April when he attended a chapter meeting of the Order of the Garter. A few days later four of the commissioners returned to England with those involved in the Botolf conspiracy (except the man himself) and their final report. We don't know what this report said or whether the prisoners would now implicate Lisle. On May Day other detainees followed – those the commissioners had found guilty of heresy. They were sent to the Fleet prison but not before they had seen Cromwell who ordered their shackles be taken off and told them to 'be of good cheer, for, if God sent him life, they should shortly go home with as much honesty, as they came with shame'.[18]

This statement was made by Foxe in his *Book of Martyrs* and if true, could be seen as Cromwell's direct intervention to protect and free those reformers. They would indeed be released but not until some months later when Audley, Lord Chancellor, told them:

I am commanded by the Council to tell you, that you are discharged by virtue of the king's general pardon; but that pardon excepteth and forbiddeth all sacramentaries, and the most part, or all of you, are called sacramentaries: therefore I cannot see how that pardon doth you any pleasure. But pray for the king's highness, for his grace's pleasure is, that I should dismiss you; and so I do, and pity you all.[19]

By this time Lisle was in trouble. He spent a month in London attending Parliament on eight occasions before his arrest on 19 May. Did he see it coming? He wrote eight letters to Honor before his imprisonment that might have given us a clue, but they are not extant. There are only two accounts of Lisle's arrest. The first comes from Elis Gruffudd, the Welsh chronicler who wrote of his downfall:

At this time, the next Whitsun holiday, Lord Lisle and his friends in Calais were given to think that he would be made an earl and that he was sent to Windsor to keep the feast of St George and that he would be the chief of the feast. The contrary indeed was true. For none of the great men of the Council looked at him save askance, for they saw that he was besmutted in some way or other, for secretly he had been before the Council once or twice, and on Whit Tuesday the Council called a meeting to discuss the matter. Here were the two dukes [Norfolk and Suffolk], the Earl of Essex, the Chancellor of the Kingdom, and others of the Council. Some say that the King was there in person; but such witnesses spoke against him [Lisle] that he was unable to go against them, for he went down on his knees and appealed to the King to help him in his righteousness. But the King told him, 'Doest thou not ask for righteousness! For I shall take trouble to hear this matter myself.' At this the lord asked the King to be merciful and righteous to him. To these words the King turned his back and went to his room without letting him answer either good or bad. The Council then sent him in the custody of Sir William Kingston, who delivered him to the Lieutenant within the walls of the Tower, around eleven at night.[20]

Lisle at least was committed into the care of his lifelong friend Sir William Kingston who must have shown him respect and perhaps even commiserated with him. But he would not be under his care for long. Kingston died at his beloved Painswick in October of the same year and Sir John Gage took over his role as Constable of the Tower.

Gruffudd wrote his version of events many years after they occurred. As a member of the Calais garrison he certainly had his ear to the ground and would know pertinent details, even if he was not always correct with dates and times. Marillac, the French ambassador, however, was in London at the time and, writing to the Constable of France, Montmorency, gave his account:

> Two days ago, at ten o'clock at night, my lord Lisle, Deputy of Calais, uncle of this king, was led prisoner to the Tower, where before had been committed three of his servants, and similarly today a chaplain of his who is come out of Flanders in a ship. The cause thereof hath not yet been so certified unto me that I can write it for truth; but it is bruited that he is accused of having had secret intelligence with the Cardinal Pole who is his near relative, and of other practices to deliver up to him the town of Calais. Howsoever it may be, the said Lord Lisle is in a very strait prison, and from the which none escape save by miracle. There have been taken also to the same place ten or twelve soldiers of the said town of Calais, who have charged the said Deputy with certain words spoken by him contrary to the honour and the faith he oweth to the King, his master.[21]

Marillac did not know why Lisle had been arrested but Gruffudd believed it was because of 'secret intelligence' – however remote – with Cardinal Pole. Further accounts mention the Botolf conspiracy and the Calais prisoners and given that this came after the Damplip affair, it was a further instance of a connection, however spurious, with Reginald Pole.

The historian J.J. Scarisbrick, writing in an online article, has posited that the plot to take Calais was just the tip of the iceberg. Once taken, papal troops would travel to England, kill the king and free the Countess of Salisbury from the Tower. It does appear that there was some substance to this. Reginald Pole, on writing to the bishop of Lavaur, mentions both his mother and a friend – namely Botolf.

As to what you write of my affairs, both what was lovingly planned for my mother's release and about that friend of ours who procured this, who afterwards on the shameless demand made by the enemy's letters was kept in custody, although you relate that he has since been liberated.[22]

Scarisbrick also names Lisle as Botolf's co-conspirator but there is no evidence to prove this. In all the depositions taken at the time there is no mention of Lisle having any knowledge of what was happening, and it is highly unlikely he would ever have been involved in a plot to kill his nephew. If he had been and there was any evidence he would have been charged and executed. It is more likely that the king, who feared Pole's influence with the Pope and hated him with every fibre of his being, saw Lisle as another one of the family he was determined to destroy. At the time Lisle was incarcerated, his cousin Margaret, Countess of Salisbury, was also there awaiting her fate.

The editor of the *Lisle Letters*, St Clare Byrne, believed Cromwell was wholly responsible for Lisle's fall from grace and had framed Lisle so he could free the Sacramentarians. While Cromwell undoubtedly had a hand in the events in Calais and was negligent in his responses to the Lord Deputy, the king was ultimately the decider of Lisle's fate.

Interestingly, in some papers that were sent to the Privy Council in London concerning Lisle there is also mention of a letter he sent to the Emperor, Charles V, through the Captain of Gravelines. Sir Thomas Wyatt mentioned it in correspondence with Cromwell and felt that Lisle had written it:

I suppose, not without knowledge of the King or the Council, but without participation with me of anything of the matter.[23]

It doesn't appear that the letter contained anything suspicious and Thomas Larke, one of Lisle's secretaries, believed it had concerned one of Calais' men-at-arms, Thomas Boyes, who had his horses detained at St Omer, but now any and every thing would be scrutinised for signs of Lisle's treason.

Henry was not convinced of his uncle's disloyalty however, or his part in any plot. There was enough suspicion to land him in prison but he was not put on trial. Ten days after Lisle's arrest the king declared he could not believe his uncle had erred of malice. But he did think he had erred in some way.

The chronicler and Welsh soldier Gruffudd made the point that explains Lisle's consequent treatment. The king declared he would deal with the matter of his uncle himself. Not the Council, the Lord Privy Seal or anyone else. That Henry perceived Reginald Pole as a threat cannot be underestimated, but any connection between Lisle and Pole or any conspiracy was obviously not forthcoming. Henry had killed many people for less but Lisle remained in the Tower without interrogation or trial.

On 30 May Cromwell ordered Sussex in Calais to search Lisle's house and question his household looking for evidence against him. Lisle's household of fifty-six people was dissolved on 2 June and his goods inventoried. Nothing was left unaccounted for. The inventory lists the contents of each room including the chapel, the cellar, the kitchen and spicery, the chambers and their chests, the storehouse, the armoury and the stable. As well as that, Lisle's plate, gold and jewels including gold chains, pearls, diamonds, rings set with rubies, emeralds and sapphires and gold buttons were listed.

Lisle's wife, Honor, and her daughters Philippa and Mary, were also placed under house arrest in Calais. Gruffudd tell us:

She, after the Council had conversed a little with her, was put in prison in a room of the Palace and the girls were taken from her and put in prison in various places through the town. At this time the Treasurer took possession of all the treasure and clothes of Lord and Lady Lisle in the King's name. From this rose various tales and great talk in the court, in London and in Calais.[24]

Marillac thought Honor would be sent over to London for questioning but instead she was kept at Francis Hall's home while investigations continued. Many blamed her for Lisle's undoing and rumours abounded as to what happened, even to the point of accusations she had been in love with Gregory Sweet-Lips.

It didn't help that another situation came to light involving her daughter Mary. Honor had received a proposal from Gabriel de Montmorency, Seigneur de Bours, a young French nobleman, to marry her daughter and for this to happen they would require the king's permission. There is no doubt Honor would have gone through the correct channels, but events had spiralled out of control and when she and her daughter were examined it was realised that Mary had secretly already become betrothed to Montmorency. Depositions were taken from anyone who had evidence and it was found that Mary had destroyed correspondence by casting letters into the jakes (toilet). To destroy evidence was incriminating and when Mary was examined for a second time she admitted she had 'contracted matrimony … and declared the same unto her sisters and to her mother'.[25] So Honor had known of the secret betrothal and they had all tried to conceal it. Although it seems that Lord Lisle had not known of the affair it was a strike against the family and it is not surprising that she 'fell distraught of mind, and so continued many years after'.[26]

Lisle was still not charged, nor did he stand trial. The king, who had said he would deal with his uncle, left him in the Tower while more important situations – to him at least – developed.

There is a story that as Cromwell left parliament on 10 June his hat blew off in the wind. It was usual for those present to doff their caps in respect, but no one moved to remove their hats. At the Council meeting that followed he walked into a subdued room where all his colleagues were seated. Going to take his place Norfolk broke the silence: 'Cromwell, do not sit there; that is no place for thee. Traitors do not sit amongst gentlemen.' He was arrested by the captain of the guard and stripped of his garter seal and insignia before being taken to the Tower of London.

The accusations against Cromwell were long and varied. As was the Tudor way once a man had been arrested and a case was being built against him that would end with his execution, the list of what he had supposedly done grew and grew. This was not happening in Lisle's case but the Lord Privy Seal was not so lucky. Cromwell was being accused of heresy, treason, corruption and plotting against the king. Some historians have hotly disputed whether there was really an anti-Cromwell faction at court to bring him down and that the Duke of Norfolk and Stephen Gardiner were responsible for engineering his fall, but we do know that once Henry decided he wanted a person gone, it was done – and ultimately it was the king that decided his fate.

On 12 June Cromwell wrote a long letter to Henry from the tower. It covered all he had been accused of including:

Sir, as to your Commonwealth, I have after my wit, power and knowledge travailed therein, doing my duty to the same having no respect to persons (your Majesty only excepted), and I trust God shall bear me witness that the world cannot justly accuse me of having done any injustice or wrong wilfully. And yet I have not done my duty in all things as I was bound, wherefore I ask mercy. If I have heard of any combinations, conventicles or offenders against your laws, I have for the most part revealed them and also caused them to be punished, not of malice, as God shall judge me. Nevertheless, Sire, I have meddled in so many matters under your Highness that I am not able to answer them all – but one thing I am well assured of is that that I have never wittingly or willingly thought to offend your Highness. Still, hard it is for me or any other meddling as I have done to live under your Grace and your laws, but we must daily offend, and where I have offended, I most humbly ask mercy and pardon at your gracious will and pleasure.[27]

On 19 June an act of attainder was passed declaring Cromwell guilty with no recourse to a trial and on 28 July he was publicly beheaded on Tower Hill. His fall had been swift and brutal. What must Lisle have felt at the news? Fear that he would be next? Hope that with Cromwell gone he may be freed? It must have been a confusing and frustrating time for him, and one that would endure for many months.

On the same day that Cromwell died, Henry married Catherine Howard secretly at Oatlands Palace. Catherine was the daughter of Lord Edmund Howard, the previous Comptroller of Calais, and Joyce Culpepper, but after her mother's death had been raised in the Dowager Duchess of Norfolk's undisciplined household. She had joined Anne of Cleves' household in January and the king had soon become besotted with her. Marillac, writing at the time, said she:

had everything necessary not only to content the king her lord, but also to win the hearts of his subjects; for, apart from her excellent beauty in which she surpassed all the ladies in England ... she has a very gentle face, gracious of speech, her bearing moderate, restrained and her conversation humane.[28]

But the king's fifth wife would later be accused of adultery and lose her life with one blow of the executioner's axe.

The king obviously was caught up in his own affairs and had made it clear that he would deal with Lisle personally but his concern about his uncle was not a priority. As well as that there was a huge volume of correspondence – Lisle's and Cromwell's – that needed to be gone through for evidence of either of their misdoings, and that would take time. Key letters that may have explained why Lisle was continually kept a prisoner are thought to be missing, put to one side by the examiners and not returned to the Lisle correspondence. The one thing that Lisle did know as he sat in his room at the Tower was that he was not going back to Calais. At the beginning of June Lord Maltravers became the new deputy and took up residence in what was once Lisle's home.

Lisle's debts were looked into on the king's orders. Gruffudd mentions he had many debts in Calais and three times as much in England. There was also Honor's keep to be paid to Francis Hall and Lisle's expenses to be covered while he was in the Tower. Accounts extant show there wasn't the money coming in to pay for all these. Byrne estimates that a seventy-two week stay in the Tower would amount to £138, but only £72 was paid out of Lisle's revenue. Was Henry footing the bill to make sure his uncle was still well cared for?

On 1 March 1541 the Privy Council met to discuss Lisle, but it was on a much more positive note – the provision of clothing for him. John Malt, the king's tailor, was to make several items, including a large gown of damask furred with black coney, two doublets of satin and a long night gown furred with black lamb, as well as six pairs of shoes. The fact that he needed six pairs of shoes shows that he could not have been solely confined to his rooms.

Interestingly, the bill of attainder that listed the men caught up in the Botolf affair originally had Lord Lisle's name on it, but somehow – by the king's command – it was expunged from the list. Whether Lisle knew it or not, he had had a close shave with death.

One who would not be so lucky was Margaret Pole, Countess of Salisbury. She had also been provided with clothing in the same bill as

Lisle, including a furred nightgown, a gown of saye (woollen cloth), lined and faced with satin, a furred petticoat and four pairs of shoes. Margaret had spent over two years in the Tower and is thought to have written on her prison wall:

> For traitors on the block should die;
> I am no traitor, no, not I!
> My faithfulness stands fast and so,
> towards the block I shall not go!
> Nor make one step, as you shall see;
> Christ in Thy Mercy, save Thou me![29]

Now aged and frail, she was given just an hour's notice her end was nigh. She truly did not believe Henry would kill her. There was no proof of any wrongdoing, there had been no trial, but on 27 May she was executed. The 67-year-old suffered a horrendous, botched execution by a 'blundering youth' who 'hacked her head and shoulders to pieces'.[30] And it was needless. She posed no threat to Henry. Chapuys made the point that 'there was no need or haste to bring so ignominious a death upon her', and given her age she would not 'in the ordinary course of nature live long'. Marillac too was shocked, 'as she had been long prisoner, was of noble lineage, above 80 years old [Marillac was mistaken about her age], and had been punished by the loss of one son and banishment of the other, and the total ruin of her house.'[31] Her death shocked the nation and Lisle, who may have seen his cousin in the Tower and at least knew she was there, must have feared that it would be his turn next.

In another sad twist to Henry's persecution of the Pole family, Margaret's grandson Henry had also been confined to the Tower at the time of his father Lord Montagu's arrest. He was last recorded as still being there in 1542 in a bill for food provision. At the time of his grandmother's execution, Chapuys wrote that he had had permission to exercise in the precincts of the Tower but after 'was placed in close confinement, and it is supposed that he will soon follow his father and grandmother. God help him!'[32] Like the Princes in the Tower, we have no more clues as to what happened to him. All record of Henry vanished, his fate unknown.

By June, Marillac had heard a rumour that Lisle was also 'in great danger to die'.[33] He had heard that the Tower was to be cleared of its prisoners, 'all will be despatched, either by condemnation or absolution' before the king went on progress. But he reported more favourably in July that it was said Lisle 'shall be kept prisoner in the Tower for his life, where he is somewhat more at large than he formerly was'.[34] We hear nothing of Lisle from any other source and it is Marillac that tells us on 17 January 1542:

> The Deputy of Calais, the Lord Lisle, who hath been a prisoner in the Tower these two years, is at a point to have his pardon, and the saying is that his Order of the Garter hath been restored to him, and known for a truth that he hath the freedom of the said Tower, where formerly he had naught but one small chamber, very narrow.[35]

Gruffudd years later echoed Lisle's freedom of movement with a story that may well be anecdotal:

> The King's Grace moved down the river in his barge from York Place to Greenwich, and at the time Lord Lisle his uncle, who was a bastard of King Edward IV, raised his hands high, and shouted hoarsely from the Tower where he was imprisoned for mercy and release from prison. The King took it graciously and sent his secretary to the Tower to the Lord to show him the King had given him his pardon and that he would have his freedom and release from prison two or three days later and that he would get back his possessions and offices.[36]

The king may have decided to let Lisle go free – and why we have no clue – except that there was never any concrete evidence of wrongdoing. There was no legal case against him but as we know that didn't mean charges couldn't have been trumped up and any legalities overruled if Henry wanted him dead. There was also no official pardon because Lisle had not been formally attainted.

Sir Thomas Wriothesley, now the king's secretary, was sent:

> To go unto him, and to deliver him a ring, with a rich diamond, for a token from him, and to tell him to be of good cheer, for although in that so weighty a matter he would not have done less to him if he

had been his own son, yet now upon thorough trial had, sith it was manifestly proved that he was void of all offence, he was sorry that he had been occasioned so far to try his truth, and therefore willed him to be of good cheer and comfort, for he should find that he would make account of him as of his most true and faithful kinsman, and not only restore him to his former liberty but otherwise further be ready to pleasure him in what he could.[37]

But it all came too late. Before Lisle had a chance to leave the Tower his heart failed him after 'the King sent him his Ring from his own Finger, with such comfortable Expressions, that he immoderately receiving so great a pressure of Joy, his heart was overcharged therewith.'[38] After seven years of trial in Calais and two in the Tower, Lisle was dead. As Sandford shrewdly put it 'this King's Mercy was as fatal as his Judgements'.[39] Lisle was laid to rest at the Tower and the costs of his funeral paid by the king, but there was no great procession or service. We don't know if anyone of import attended his interment and his resting place in the royal chapel of St Peter ad Vincula was not even marked. Why when he had been granted his liberty, was he buried like a criminal?

Honor and some of their children were still in Calais and had heard the news he was to be set free and might return as deputy, but just as swiftly news came of his demise. Orders were sent for Honor's house arrest to end and her clothes and jewels to be returned. This is noted in a Privy Council meeting in March. Apart from Marillac reporting to Francis I, 'Lord Lisle, formerly deputy of Calais, being out of trouble and his Order, honour and goods restored, died a few days afterwards',[40] there is no other mention in the Letters and Papers of Lisle's demise. It was a sad and unfitting end for the illegitimate son of Edward IV.

Henry would reign for another five years, slowly devolving into an obese tyrant. He was ultimately responsible for his uncle's death – the man he had once said had 'the gentlest heart living'.

Epilogue

Calais came under siege in 1557. Henry VIII's daughter Mary was now queen and she had married Philip of Spain who involved England in war with Henri II of France. Henri ordered the Duke of Guise to launch a surprise attack to retake the town with a vast army of 30,000 men. Outnumbered and completely overwhelmed by the siege, Calais surrendered on 7 January 1558. It is said that when Queen Mary was dying, she told her ladies: 'When I am dead and cut open, they will find Philip and Calais inscribed on my heart.'

Honor had long returned to England, never marrying again; her own death came twenty-four years later. It is possible that she had Lisle reinterred at Soberton. A later reference to the church there stated he was buried in the south transept, but this can't be proved. It would be nice to think that after all his trials, he finally found a peaceful resting place.

Lisle's daughters Frances, Elizabeth and Bridget, all made marriages befitting their status. Frances married her stepbrother John Basset in 1538, and after his death married Thomas Monck from Devon. By John Basset she had two children: Honor born in 1539 and Arthur born in 1541 after his father's death. By her second husband she had six children: Margaret, Anthony, John, Francis, Catherine and Mary.

Frances' grandson, and Lisle's great-grandson, Robert Basset made a claim to the throne after Queen Elizabeth I's death which resulted in the sale of thirty of the family's manors to pay his heavy fine:

> Sir Robert Basset, by his grandmother, descended from the Plantagenets, and of the blood royal, in the beginning of King James's reign, made some pretensions to the crown of England; but, not being able to make them good, was forced to fly into France to save his head; to compound for which, together with his generous way of living, he greatly exhausted his estate, selling off no less than

thirty manors of land; though there is now a fair estate belonging to the heir of the family.[1]

Elizabeth had stayed in England in the care of her half-brother Sir John Dudley while her father was in Calais. At around the age of 16 a marriage to Sir Frances Lovell's son Thomas was arranged for her, but it did not go through. She later married Sir Francis Jobson, one of Dudley's secretaries, with whom she had five children: John, Edward, Thomas, Henry and Mary, who said:

> I was married to my wife at the request of the duke, he promising that he would help me to a manor that my Lord Windsor had in Staffordshire; being disappointed of the said manor he borrowed a good part of my money.[2]

When her husband was Lieutenant of the Tower, Elizabeth often stayed with him although their main residence was in Colchester, but in 1569 she grew gravely ill. There is a story that Queen Elizabeth sent her physician Burchard Kranich, who had treated her for smallpox, to examine Elizabeth, but he could only make her more comfortable in her last days. When the end came, she died with a book in her hand, reading.

Bridget had been schooled at St Mary's Abbey in Winchester, under the care of Dame Elizabeth Shelley, the abbess. One of her childhood companions was Mary Pole, the daughter of Geoffrey Pole. When the abbey was dissolved Bridget moved on to Sir Anthony Windsor's household in November 1538:

> I allowed your daughter Mistress Bryggett to Sir Antony Windsor's to sport her for a week. And because she was out of apparel, that Master Windsor might see her, I was the better content to let her go; and since that time she came no more at Winchester, wherein I beseech your ladyship think no unkindness in me for my light sending of her; for if I had not esteemed her to have come again, she should not have comen there at that time.[3]

At the end of the same year it seems that when Honor was in England, she collected Bridget to take her back to Calais, although it seems that

Lisle was not impressed. We rarely have any insight into how Lisle treated his daughters, but he must have got on well with Frances who lived with him. Elizabeth he never saw and Bridget, it appears, he didn't want to. In a letter to his wife he added a postscript: 'there is no man living would gladlier have his wife's company then I would have yours ... I am sorry that ye will bring my daughter Bridget with you.'[4] Bridget was sent away to a convent but she later married William Carden or Cawarden, a gentleman with lands in Kent.

And finally John Husee, he who had supported Lisle, Honor and their extended family during their stay in Calais remained in the garrison after Lisle's fall. He had been granted the role of searcher of Marke and Oye for life and he continued with his duties, also serving the English army in 1544, organising supplies for the siege of Boulogne. He does not appear to have married and there is no mention of any children. He spent his life serving his master and his king. Husee died in November 1548, six years after Lisle, the man to whom he had devoted his life.

References

Chapter One

1. Ross, *Edward IV*, p. 10
2. Ross, *Edward IV*, p. 86
3. Ross, *Edward IV*, p. 89
4. Ross, *Edward IV*, p. 315
5. Ross, *Edward IV*, p. 86
6. Ross, *Edward IV*, p. 86
7. Vergil, *Anglica Historia*, https://archive.org/details/threebooksofpoly29verg
8. More, *History of Richard III*, https://archive.org/details/moreshistoryofki00 morerich
9. Buck, *History of the Life and Reigne of Richard III*, https://archive.org/details/historyofliferei00buckuoft
10. Ashdown-Hill, *The Private Life of Edward IV*, p. 162
11. More, *History of Richard III*, https://archive.org/details/moreshistoryofki00 morerich
12. Ibid
13. Ibid
14. Amin, *Henry VII and the Tudor Pretenders*, p. 27
15. Buck, *History of the Life and Reigne of Richard III*, https://archive.org/details/historyofliferei00buckuoft
16. Ashdown-Hill, *The Private Life of Edward IV*, p. 143
17. Calendar of Close Rolls, Edward IV: Volume 2, 1468–1476
18. Scofield, *Edward IV*, Vol 2, p. 56
19. Given-Wilson, *The Royal Bastards of Medieval England*, p. 161
20. Richardson, *Plantagenet Ancestry: A Study In Colonial And Medieval Families*, p. 583
21. Richardson, *Plantagenet Ancestry: A Study In Colonial And Medieval Families*, p. 584
22. Ross, *Edward IV*, p. 10
23. Commynes, *Memoirs: the reign of Louis XI 1461–1483*, pp. 353–354
24. Lingard, *The History of England*, p. 235
25. More, *History of Richard III*, https://archive.org/details/moreshistoryofki00 morerich
26. Cannon, *The Oxford Illustrated History of the British*, p. 37
27. *Calendar of Close Rolls – Richard III*
28. Vergil, *Anglica Historia*, https://archive.org/details/threebooksofpoly29verg

29. Chrimes, *Henry VII*, p. 51
30. Horrox, *The Parliament Rolls of Medieval England,1275 –1504*
31. Elizabeth of York's Privy Purse expenses, 1502 –1503
32. Crawford, *Letters of the Queens of England, 1100–1547*, p. 150
33. Hall, *Hall's Chronicle: Containing the history of England,* https://archive.org/details/hallschronicleco00hall
34. Heneage Jesse, Memoirs of King Richard III, p. 159
35. Hall, *Hall's Chronicle: Containing the history of England,* https://archive.org/details/hallschronicleco00hall

Chapter Two
1. Hall, *Hall's Chronicle: Containing the history of England,* https://archive.org/details/hallschronicleco00hall
2. Hutchinson, *Young Henry*, p. 137
3. *CSP Venice*
4. *Lisle Letters*, vol 1, p. 158
5. *Letters and Papers, Foreign and Domestic, Henry VIII*
6. Hall, *Hall's Chronicle: Containing the history of England,* https://archive.org/details/hallschronicleco00hall
7. *CSP Venice*
8. Hall, *Hall's Chronicle: Containing the history of England,* https://archive.org/details/hallschronicleco00hall
9. Ibid
10. Ibid
11. Holinshed, *Chronicles of England, Scotland and Ireland*, p. 688
12. *Lisle Letters*, vol 1, p. 165
13. *Letters and Papers, Foreign and Domestic, Henry VIII*
14. *Lisle Letters*, vol 1, p. 177
15. *Lisle Letters*, vol 1, p. 256
16. Leland, *De Rebus Brittanicis Collectanea*
17. *Lisle Letters*, vol 1, p. 183
18. *Lisle Letters*, vol 1, p.186
19. *Lisle Letters*, vol 1, p. 189
20. Leviticus 20:21
21. *Letters and Papers, Foreign and Domestic, Henry VIII*
22. *Letters and Papers, Foreign and Domestic, Henry VIII*
23. *Lisle Letters*, vol 1, p. 217
24. *Lisle Letters*, vol 1, p. 218
25. Ibid
26. Ibid
27. *Letters and Papers, Foreign and Domestic, Henry VIII*
28. *Letters and Papers, Foreign and Domestic, Henry VIII*
29. *Lisle Letters*, vol 1, p. 251
30. *Lisle Letters*, vol 1, p. 254

Chapter Three
1. Froissart's Chroncile
2. Morris, *In the Footsteps of Anne Boleyn*, p. 103
3. Grummitt, *The Calais Garrison*, p. 1
4. *Lisle Letters*, vol 1, p. 457
5. Hall, *Hall's Chronicle: Containing the history of England*, https://archive.org/details/hallschronicleco00hall
6. Ibid
7. *Lisle Letters*, vol 1, p. 466
8. Rose, *Calais: An English Town in France 1347–1558*, p. 119
9. Nichols, *The Chronicle of Calais*, p. 125
10. *Lisle Letters*, vol 1, p. 478
11. Nichols, *The Chronicle of Calais*, p. 141
12. *Lisle Letters*, vol 1, p. 445
13. *Lisle Letters*, vol 1, p. 530
14. *Letters and Papers, Foreign and Domestic, Henry VIII*
15. Bush, 'The Lisle-Seymour Land Disputes'
16. *Lisle Letters*, vol 1, p. 595
17. *Lisle Letters*, vol 1, p. 596
18. *Letters and Papers, Foreign and Domestic, Henry VIII*
19. *Lisle Letters*, vol 1, p. 510
20. *Letters and Papers, Foreign and Domestic, Henry VIII*
21. Ibid
22. Weir, *Six Wives of Henry VIII*, p. 258
23. *Lisle Letters*, vol 1, p. 552
24. Ibid
25. Ibid
26. *Lisle Letters*, vol 1, p. 592
27. Potter, 'The Private Face of Anglo-French Relations in the Sixteenth-Century' p. 200
28. *Lisle Letters*, vol 1, p. 561
29. *Lisle Letters*, vol 1, p. 599
30. *Lisle Letters*, vol 1, p. 599
31. *Lisle Letters*, vol 1, p. 598
32. *Lisle Letters*, vol 1, p. 601
33. *Lisle Letters*, vol 1, p. 641
34. *Lisle Letters*, vol 1, p. 642
35. *Lisle Letters*, vol 1, p. 643
36. *Lisle Letters*, vol 1, p. 648
37. *Lisle Letters*, vol 1, p. 657

Chapter Four
1. *Lisle Letters*, vol 2, p.30
2. *Lisle Letters*, vol 2, p. 54

3. *Lisle Letters*, vol 2, p. 5
4. *Lisle Letters*, vol 2, p. 43
5. *Lisle Letters*, vol 2, p. 72
6. *Lisle Letters*, vol 2, p. 113
7. *Lisle Letters*, vol 2, p. 112
8. *Lisle Letters*, vol 2, p. 87
9. *Lisle Letters*, vol 2, p. 90
10. *Lisle Letters*, vol 2, p. 91
11. *Lisle Letters*, vol 2, p. 92
12. Treason Act http://law2.umkc.edu/faculty/projects/ftrials/more/moreoath.html
13. *Lisle Letters*, vol 2, p. 116
14. Logan, *The Cambridge Companion to Thomas More*, p. 122
15. *Lisle Letters*, vol 2, p. 139
16. *CSP Spain*
17. *Lisle Letters*, vol 2, p. 145
18. *Lisle Letters*, vol 2, p. 202
19. *Lisle Letters*, vol 2, p. 179
20. *Lisle Letters*, vol 2, p. 136
21. *Lisle Letters*, vol 2, p. 240
22. Ibid
23. *Lisle Letters*, vol 2, p. 241
24. *Letters and Papers, Foreign and Domestic, Henry VIII*
25. *Lisle Letters*, vol 2, p. 258
26. *Lisle Letters*, vol 2, p. 252
27. Ibid
28. *Lisle Letters*, vol 2, p. 256
29. Ibid
30. *Lisle Letters*, vol 2, p. 267
31. *Lisle Letters*, vol 2, p. 279
32. *Lisle Letters*, vol 2, p. 310
33. *Lisle Letters*, vol 2, p. 260
34. *Lisle Letters*, vol 2, p. 261
35. *Lisle Letters*, vol 2, p. 288
36. Ibid
37. *Lisle Letters*, vol 2, p. 289
38. *Lisle Letters*, vol 2, p. 294
39. *Lisle Letters*, vol 2, p. 299
40. *Lisle Letters*, vol 2, p. 307
41. *Lisle Letters*, vol 2, p. 308
42. *Lisle Letters*, vol 2, p. 317
43. *Lisle Letters*, vol 2, p. 321

Chapter Five
1. *Lisle Letters*, vol 2, p. 388
2. *Lisle Letters*, vol 2, p. 389
3. *Lisle Letters*, vol 2, p. 440
4. *Lisle Letters*, vol 2, p. 438
5. *Letters and Papers, Foreign and Domestic, Henry VIII*
6. *Lisle Letters*, vol 2, p. 440
7. *Lisle Letters*, vol 2, p. 381
8. *Lisle Letters*, vol 2, p. 488
9. *Lisle Letters*, vol 2, p. 489
10. Ibid
11. *Lisle Letters*, vol 2, p. 499
12. *Lisle Letters*, vol 2, p. 479
13. *Lisle Letters*, vol 2, p. 536
14. Ibid
15. *CSP Spain*
16. Treason Act http://law2.umkc.edu/faculty/projects/ftrials/more/moreoath. html
17. Hall, *Hall's Chronicle: Containing the history of England*, https://archive.org/details/hallschronicleco00hall
18. *Lisle Letters*, vol 2, p. 515
19. Ibid
20. *Lisle Letters*, vol 2, p. 516
21. *Lisle Letters*, vol 2, p. 529
22. Ibid
23. *Lisle Letters*, vol 2, p. 550
24. *Lisle Letters*, vol 2, p. 553
25. *Chronicles of Calais*, p. 130
26. Grummitt, *The English Experience in France c. 1450–1558*, p. 46
27. *Lisle Letters*, vol 1, p. 448
28. Ibid
29. Graves, *Early Tudor Parliaments 1485–1558*, p. 89
30. Statutes of the Realm, vol 3, p. 200
31. *Lisle Letters*, vol 2, p. 596
32. *Lisle Letters*, vol 2, p. 614
33. Ibid
34. *Lisle Letters*, vol 2, p. 615
35. *Lisle Letters*, vol 2, p. 656
36. *Lisle Letters*, vol 2, p. 657

Chapter Six
1. *CSP Spain*
2. *Lisle Letters*, vol 3, p. 256
3. *Lisle Letters*, vol 3, p. 165

4. *Lisle Letters*, vol 3, p. 318
5. Ibid
6. *Lisle Letters*, vol 3, p. 336
7. *Lisle Letters*, vol 3, p. 335
8. *Lisle Letters*, vol 3, p. 312
9. *CSP Spain*
10. *Letters and Papers, Foreign and Domestic, Henry VIII*
11. *Lisle Letters*, vol 3, p. 358
12. https://englishhistory.net/tudor/queen-anne-boleyn-letter-king-henry-viii/
13. Ives, *The Life and Death of Anne Boleyn*, p. 341
14. *Lisle Letters*, vol 3, p. 361
15. *Lisle Letters*, vol 3, p. 371
16. *Lisle Letters*, vol 3, p. 372
17. *Lisle Letters*, vol 3, p. 378
18. Hardy, *Documents Illustrative of English Church History*, p. 257.
19. *Lisle Letters*, vol 3, p. 420
20. *Lisle Letters*, vol 3, p. 426
21. *Lisle Letters*, vol 3, p. 435
22. *Lisle Letters*, vol 3, p. 453
23. *Lisle Letters*, vol 3, p. 469
24. Ibid
25. *Lisle Letters*, vol 3, p. 473
26. *Lisle Letters*, vol 3, p. 500
27. Fletcher, *Tudor Rebellions*, p. 106
28. *Lisle Letters*, vol 3, p. 572
29. *Lisle Letters*, vol 3, p. 539
30. *Lisle Letters*, vol 3, p. 551
31. *Lisle Letters*, vol 3, p. 553
32. *Lisle Letters*, vol 3, p. 566
33. *Letters and Papers, Foreign and Domestic, Henry VIII*
34. *Lisle Letters*, vol 3, p. 576

Chapter Seven
1. *Lisle Letters*, vol 4, p. 232
2. *Lisle Letters*, vol 4, p. 233
3. *Letters and Papers, Foreign and Domestic, Henry VIII*
4. *Lisle Letters*, vol 4, p. 231
5. *Lisle Letters*, vol 4, p. 242
6. *Lisle Letters*, vol 4, p. 234
7. Schenk, *Reginald Pole*, p. 71
8. Higginbotham, *Margaret Pole: The Countess in the Tower*, p. 111
9. *Letters and Papers, Foreign and Domestic, Henry VIII*
10. *Letters and Papers, Foreign and Domestic, Henry VIII*

11. Higginbotham, *Margaret Pole: The Countess in the Tower*, p. 113
12. *CSP Spain*
13. *Letters and Papers, Foreign and Domestic, Henry VIII*
14. *Letters and Papers, Foreign and Domestic, Henry VIII*
15. *Lisle Letters*, vol 4, p. 288
16. Ibid
17. *Lisle Letters*, vol 4, p. 294
18. Pierce, *Margaret Pole*, p. 101
19. *CSP Spain*
20. Pierce, *Margaret Pole*, p. 102
21. Pierce, *Margaret Pole*, p. 70
22. *Lisle Letters*, vol 4, p. 140
23. *Lisle Letters*, vol 4, p. 296
24. *Lisle Letters*, vol 4, p. 297
25. *Lisle Letters*, vol 4, p. 298
26. *Lisle Letters*, vol 4, p. 331
27. *Lisle Letters*, vol 4, p. 311
28. *Lisle Letters*, vol 4, p. 383
29. *Lisle Letters*, vol 4, p. 347
30. Ibid
31. *Lisle Letters*, vol 4, p. 349
32. *Lisle Letters*, vol 4, p. 357
33. *Lisle Letters*, vol 4, p. 359
34. *Lisle Letters*, vol 4, p. 360
35. *Lisle Letters*, vol 4, p. 363
36. *Lisle Letters*, vol 4, p. 372
37. *Lisle Letters*, vol 4, p. 374
38. *Lisle Letters*, vol 4, p. 378
39. *Lisle Letters*, vol 4, p. 403
40. *Lisle Letters*, vol 4, p. 425
41. *Lisle Letters*, vol 4, p. 159
42. *Lisle Letters*, vol 4, p. 169
43. *Lisle Letters*, vol 4, p. 432
44. *Lisle Letters*, vol 4, p. 441

Chapter Eight
1. *Lisle Letters*, vol 5, p. 19
2. *Lisle Letters*, vol 5, p. 30
3. *Lisle Letters*, vol 5, p. 38
4. *Lisle Letters*, vol 5, p. 40
5. *Lisle Letters*, vol 5, p. 53
6. *Lisle Letters*, vol 5, p. 54
7. *Lisle Letters*, vol 4, p. 83
8. *Lisle Letters*, vol 5, p. 63

9. *Lisle Letters*, vol 5, p. 66
10. *Lisle Letters*, vol 5, p. 80
11. *Lisle Letters*, vol 5, p. 97
12. *Lisle Letters*, vol 5, p. 108
13. *Lisle Letters*, vol 5, p. 114
14. *Lisle Letters*, vol 5, p. 152
15. *Lisle Letters*, vol 5, p. 178
16. Wall, *Shrines of British Saints*, p. 238
17. *Lisle Letters*, vol 5, p. 125
18. *Lisle Letters*, vol 5, p. 136
19. Ibid
20. *Lisle Letters*, vol 5, p. 256
21. *Lisle Letters*, vol 5, p. 230
22. *Lisle Letters*, vol 5, p. 231
23. *Lisle Letters*, vol 5, p. 259
24. *Lisle Letters*, vol 5, p. 283
25. *Lisle Letters*, vol 5, p. 289
26. *Lisle Letters*, vol 5, p. 316
27. *Letters and Papers, Foreign and Domestic, Henry VIII*
28. Pierce, *Margaret Pole*, p. 119
29. *Letters and Papers, Foreign and Domestic, Henry VIII*
30. *Lisle Letters*, vol 5, p. 266
31. *Letters and Papers, Foreign and Domestic, Henry VIII*
32. Ibid
33. Pierce, *Margaret Pole*, p. 132
34. *Letters and Papers, Foreign and Domestic, Henry VIII*
35. Ibid
36. Ibid
37. *Lisle Letters*, vol 5, p. 324
38. *Lisle Letters*, vol 5, p. 320
39. *Letters and Papers, Foreign and Domestic, Henry VIII*
40. Pierce, *Margaret Pole*, p. 140
41. *Lisle Letters*, vol 5, p. 331
42. *Lisle Letters*, vol 5, p. 335
43. *Lisle Letters*, vol 5, p. 345

Chapter Nine
1. *Lisle Letters*, vol 5, p. 375
2. *Lisle Letters*, vol 5, p. 353
3. *Lisle Letters*, vol 5, p. 422
4. *Lisle Letters*, vol 5, p. 389
5. *Lisle Letters*, vol 5, p. 463
6. *Lisle Letters*, vol 5, p. 471
7. *Lisle Letters*, vol 5, p. 474

8. *Letters and Papers, Foreign and Domestic, Henry VIII*
9. Pierce, *Margaret Pole*, p. 173
10. Ibid
11. *Lisle Letters*, vol 5, p. 481
12. https://www.biblicalheritageexhibit.com/blogs/history-of-the-english-bible/1539-the-great-bible-the-chained-bible
13. *Lisle Letters*, vol 5, p. 489
14. Strype, Ecclesiastical Memorials, p. 436
15. Blunt, *The Reformation and the Church of England*, p. 344
17. *Lisle Letters*, vol 5, p. 500
18. *Lisle Letters*, vol 5, p. 502
19. *Letters and Papers, Foreign and Domestic, Henry VIII*
20. *Lisle Letters*, vol 5, p. 505
21. *Lisle Letters*, vol 5, p. 517
22. *Lisle Letters*, vol 5, p. 510
23. *Lisle Letters*, vol 5, p. 511
24. *Lisle Letters*, vol 5, p. 524
25. *Lisle Letters*, vol 5, p. 540
26. *Lisle Letters*, vol 5, p. 556
27. Marshall, Peter, *Heretics and Believers*, p. 27
28. *Lisle Letters*, vol 5, p. 585
29. *Foxe's Book of Martyrs*
30. *Lisle Letters*, vol 5, p. 579
31. Pierce, *Margaret Pole*, p. 177
32. *Lisle Letters*, vol 5, p. 622
33. *Foxe's Book of Martyrs*
34. *Lisle Letters*, vol 5, p. 646
35. *Lisle Letters*, vol 5, p. 655
36. *Lisle Letters*, vol 5, p. 684
37. *Lisle Letters*, vol 5, p. 699
38. *Lisle Letters*, vol 5, p. 679
39. *Letters and Papers, Foreign and Domestic, Henry VIII*
40. Ibid
41. Ibid
42. Ibid
43. *Lisle Letters*, vol 5, p. 730

Chapter Ten

1. *Letters and Papers, Foreign and Domestic, Henry*
2. *Foxe's Book of Martyrs*
3. Ibid
4. Ibid
5. Ibid
6. *Lisle Letters*, vol 5, p. 157

7. Ibid
8. *Lisle Letters*, vol 6, p. 152
9. *Lisle Letters*, vol 6, p. 163
10. Smith, *Treason in Tudor England: Politics and Paranoia*, p. 5
11. *Lisle Letters*, vol 6, p. 54
12. *Lisle Letters*, vol 6, p. 79
13. *Lisle Letters*, vol 6, p. 84
14. *Lisle Letters*, vol 6, p. 87
15. *Lisle Letters*, vol 6, p. 87
16. *Lisle Letters*, vol 6, p. 92
17. *Lisle Letters*, vol 6, p. 106
18. *Lisle Letters*, vol 6, p. 117
19. *Foxe's Book of Martyrs*
20. *Lisle Letters*, vol 6, p. 118
21. Ibid
22. https://catholicherald.co.uk/the-plot-to-depose-henry-viii/
23. *Letters and Papers, Foreign and Domestic, Henry*
24. *Lisle Letters*, vol 6, p. 139
25. *Lisle Letters*, vol 6, p. 147
26. *Foxe's Book of Martyrs*
27. https://janetwertman.com/2015/06/12/june-12-1540-cromwells-initial-plea-to-henry-viii-full-text/
28. *Letters and Papers, Foreign and Domestic, Henry*
29. Ibid
30. *CSP Spain*
31. Pierce, *Margaret Pole*, p. 177
32. *CSP Spain*
33. *Letters and Papers, Foreign and Domestic, Henry*
34. *Lisle Letters*, vol 6, p. 176
35. *Lisle Letters*, vol 6, p. 179
36. *Lisle Letters*, vol 6, p. 180
37. Holinshed, *Chronicles of England, Scotland and Ireland*
38. *Lisle Letters*, vol 6, p. 184
39. Ibid
40. *CSP France*

Epilogue
1. Worthies of Devon
2. https://www.historyofparliamentonline.org/volume/1509-1558/member/jobson-sir-francis-1509-73
3. *Lisle Letters*, vol 5, p. 221
4. *Lisle Letters*, vol 5, p. 313

Bibliography

Amin, Nathan, *Henry VII and the Tudor Pretenders: Simnel, Warbeck, and Warwick*, Stroud, 2021

Ashdown-Hill, John, 'Lady Eleanor Talbot: New evidence, new anwsers, new questions', *The Ricardian*, Vol. 16, 2006

Ashdown-Hill, John, *The Private Life of Edward IV*, Stroud, 2017

Ashdown-Hill, John, *The Secret Queen*, Stroud, 216

Baldwin Smith, Lacey, *Treason in Tudor England*, London, 1986

Barnfield, Marie and Lark, Stephen, 'The Paternity of Lady Lumley: Some new evidence, *The Ricardian*, Vol. 26, 2016

Bernard, André, *The Life of Henry VII*, translated and introduced by Daniel Hobbins, New York, 2011

Bernard, G.W., *Anne Boleyn: Fatal Attractions*, Yale, 2010

Bernard, G.W., Thomas Cromwell and Calais, *Southampton University Website*, 1–111, 2007

Bernard, G.W., *The King's Reformation*, Yale, 2005

Bernard, G.W., *The Tudor Nobility*, Manchester, 1992

Blunt, John Henry, *The Reformation and the Church of England: Its History*, London, 1869

Borman, Tracy, *Thomas Cromwell*, London, 2014

Buck, *History of the Life and Reigne of Richard III*, https://archive.org/details/historyofliferei00buckuoft

Bush M.L., 'The Lisle-Seymour Land Disputes: A Study of Power and Influence in the 1530s', *The Historical Journal*, Vol. 9, No. 3 (1966), pp. 255–274

Calendar of Close Rolls, Edward IV: Volume 2, 1468–1476

Calendar of State Papers, Foreign

Calendar of State Papers, France

Calendar of State Papers, Spain

Calendar of State Papers, Venice

Cannon, John, Griffiths, Ralph, *The Oxford Illustrated History of the British*, Oxford, 1988

Cheney, Charles Edward, *A Belated Plantagenet*, Chicago, 1914

Chettle, H.F. 'The Burgesses for Calais, 1536–1558.' *The English Historical Review*, vol. 50, no. 199, 1935, pp. 492–501. *JSTOR*, www.jstor.org/stable/553556. Accessed 19 May 2021

Chrimes, S B, *Henry VII*, Yale, 1999

Commynes, Phillipé De, *Memoirs: the reign of Louis XI 1461–1483*, London, 1972

Crawford, Anne, *Letters of the Queens of England, 1100–1547*, London, 1994

Cripps-Day, F H, *The History of the Tournament in England and France*, London, 1918

Crosland, Margaret, *The Life and Legend of Jane Shore*, Stroud, 2006

Erickson, Carolly, *Great Harry: The Extravagant Life of Henry VIII*, London, 1997

Fletcher, Anthony, *Tudor Rebellions*, London, 1983

Foxe, John, *History of the Acts and Monuments of the Church (Foxe's Book of Martyrs)*, London, 1563

Fraser, Antonia, *The Six Wives of Henry VIII*, London, 1992

Freida, Leona, *Francis I*, London, 2018

Given-Wilson, *The Royal Bastards of Medieval England*, London, 1995

Grafton, Richard, *Grafton's Chronicle, Or History of England: To which is Added His Table of the Bailiffs, Sheriffs and Mayors of the City of London from the Year 1189, to 1558, Volumes 1 and 2*, London, 1809

Graves, Michael A.R., *Early Tudor Parliaments 1485–1558*, London, 2014

Griffiths, R.A, *The Making of the Tudor Dynasty*, Stroud, 2011

Grummitt, David, *The Calais Garrison: War and Military Service in England, 1436–1558*, Woodbridge, 2008

Grummitt, David, (ed), *The English Experience in France c.1450–1558*, London, 2002

Hall, Edward, *Hall's Chronicle: Containing the history of England*, ed. H. Ellis, London, 1809

Hanson, Marilee. 'Letter By Queen Anne Boleyn to her husband, King Henry VIII 6 May 1536' https://englishhistory.net/tudor/queen-anne-boleyn-letter-king-henry-viii/ February 10, 2015

Hardy, William John, *Documents Illustrative of English Church History*, London, 1910

Harris, Barbara J. 'Women and Politics in Early Tudor England.' *The Historical Journal*, vol. 33, no. 2, 1990, pp. 259–281. *JSTOR*, www.jstor.org/stable/2639457. Accessed 19 May 2021.

Head, David, *The Ebbs and Flows of Fortune: The Life of Thomas Howard, Third Duke of Norfolk*, Athens, 2009

Heneage Jesse, John, *Memoirs of King Richard III. and some of his contemporaries: With and historical drama on the battle of Bosworth*, London, 1862

Higginbotham, Susan, *Margaret Pole: The Countess in the Tower*, Stroud, 2016

Holinshed, Raphael, *Chronicles of England, Scotland and Ireland*, London, 1807

Horrox, Rosemary (ed.), *The Parliament Rolls of Medieval England,1275 -1504*, Vol XV, 2005

Hutchinson, Robert, *House of Treason: The Rise and Fall of the Tudor Dynasty*, London, 2009

Hutchinson, Robert, *Young Henry: The Rise of Henry VIII*, London, 2012

Ives, Eric, *The Life and Death of Anne Boleyn*, London, 2005

Knecht, R.J., *Francis I*, Cambridge, 1982

Letters and Papers, Foreign and Domestic, Henry VIII

Leland, *De Rebus Brittanicis Collectanea*, Vol 5, London, 1774

Licence, Amy, *Elizabeth of York*, Stroud, 2013

Lingard, John, *The History of England: From the First Invasion by the Romans to the Accession of William and Mary in 1688*, Vol 4, London 1883

Loades, David, *Henry VIII: Court, church and conflict*, The National Archives, 2007

Loades, David, *Henry VIII: King and Court*, Andover, 2009

Loades, David, *Thomas Cromwell: Servant to Henry VIII*, Stroud, 2013

Logan George M., *The Cambridge Companion to Thomas More*, Cambridge, 2011

Loughlin, Susan, *Insurrection*, Stroud, 2016

MacCulloch, Diarmaid, *All Things Made New*, London, 2017

MacCulloch, Diarmaid, *Thomas Cranmer*, New Haven & London, 1996

MacCulloch, Diarmaid, *Thomas Cromwell*, London, 2019

Mann, Catherine. 'Clothing Bodies, Dressing Rooms: Fashioning Fecundity in The Lisle Letters.' *Parergon*, vol. 22 no. 1, 2005, p. 137–157. *Project MUSE*, doi:10.1353/pgn.2005.0043.

Marshall, Peter, *Heretics and Believers: A History of the English Reformation*, New Haven & London, 2017

Mathusiak, John, *Henry VIII*, Stroud, 2013

Mattingly, Garrett, *Catherine of Aragon*, New York, 1941

Merriman, R.B., *Life and Letters of Thomas Cromwell*, Oxford, 1902

Miller, Helen, *Henry VIII and the English Nobility*, Oxford, 1989

Moorhouse, Geoffrey, *Great Harry's Navy*, London, 2005

Moorhouse, Geoffrey, *The Pilgrimage of Grace*, London, 2002

More, *History of Richard III*

Morris, Sarah and Grueninger, Natalie, *In the Footsteps of Anne Boleyn*, Stroud, 2013

Nichols, John Gough, *The Chronicle of Calais, in the reigns of Henry VII and Henry VIII to the year 1540*, J. B. Nichols and Son, 1846

Parmiter, Geoffrey de C, *The King's Great Matter*, London, 1967

Pierce, Hazel, *Margaret Pole Countess of Salisbury 1473–1541: Loyalty, Lineage and Leadership*, Cardiff, 2003

Porter, Linda, *Katherine the Queen*, London, 2010

Potter, David, 'The Private Face of Anglo-French Relations in the Sixteenth-Century: the Lisles and their French Friends, in *The English Experience in France in the 16th Century c.1450–1558: War, Diplomacy and Cultural Exchange*, D. Grummitt (ed.), Ashgate, 2002

Rappaport, Steve, *Worlds Within Worlds: Structures of Life in Sixteenth-Century London*, Cambridge, 2002

Richardson, Douglas, *Plantagenet Ancestry: A Study In Colonial And Medieval Families*, 2nd Edition, 2011

Richardson, Glenn, *The Field of the Cloth of Gold*, New Haven & London, 2020

Rose, Susan, *Calais: An English Town in France 1347–1558*, Woodbridge, 2008

Ross, Charles, *Edward IV*, London, 1983

Sandeman, G A C, *Calais Under English Rule*, Oxford, 1908

Sander, Nicholas, *Rise and Growth of the Anglican Schism*, London, 1877

Scarisbrick, J.J., *Henry VIII*, London, 1997

Schenk, W., *Reginald Pole: Cardinal of England*, London, 1950

Schofield, John, *The Rise and Fall of Thomas Cromwell*, Stroud, 2011

Sim, Alison, *Masters and Servants in Tudor England*, Stroud, 2006

Slavin, Arthur J. 'Cromwell, Cranmer and Lord Lisle: A Study in the Politics of Reform.' Albion: A Quarterly Journal Concerned with British Studies, vol. 9, no. 4, 1977, pp. 316–336, www.jstor.org/stable/4048307. Accessed 19 May 2021.

Starkey, David, *The Reign of Henry VIII*, London, 1985

Starkey, David, *Six Wives: The Queens of Henry VIII*, London, 2003

St Clare Byrne, Muriel, ed., *The Lisle Letters*, Chicago, 1981

Strype, *Ecclesiastical Memorials of Henry VIII, Edward VI and Mary*, London, 1816

Wall, J. Charles, *Shrines of British Saints*, London. 1905

Warnicke, Retha, *The Rise and Fall of Anne Boleyn: Family Politics at the Court of Henry VIII*, Cambridge, 1991

Wilson, Derek, *The English Reformation*, London, 2012

Weir, Alison, *The Lady in the Tower*, London, 2010

Weir, Alison, *The Six Wives of Henry VIII*, London, 1991

Weir, Alison, *Henry VIII: King and Court*, London, 2008

Young, Alan, *Tudor and Jacobean Tournaments*, London, 1987

Index